T0362208

International African Library 12
General editors: J. D. Y. Peel and David Parkin

RANCHING AND ENTERPRISE
IN EASTERN BOTSWANA

International African Library

General Editors

J. D. Y. Peel *and* David Parkin

The *International African Library* is a major monograph series from the International African Institute and complements its quarterly periodical *Africa*, the premier journal in the field of African studies. Theoretically informed ethnographies, studies of social relations 'on the ground' which are sensitive to local cultural forms, have long been central to the Institute's publications programme. The *IAL* maintains this strength but extends it into new areas of contemporary concern, both practical and intellectual. It includes works focused on problems of development, especially on the linkages between the local and national levels of society; studies along the interface between the social and environmental sciences; and historical studies, especially those of a social, cultural or interdisciplinary character.

Titles in the series:

Editorial Consultants

Kofi Agawu
Pierre Bonte
John Comaroff
Johannes Fabian
Paulin Hountondji
Ivan Karp
Sally Falk Moore

RANCHING AND ENTERPRISE
IN EASTERN BOTSWANA

A Case Study of
Black and White Farmers

ISAAC NCUBE MAZONDE

EDINBURGH UNIVERSITY PRESS
for the International African Institute, London

© Isaac Ncube Mazonde, 1994

Transferred to Digital Print 2010

Edinburgh University Press Ltd
22 George Square, Edinburgh

Typeset in Linotronic Plantin
by Speedspools, Edinburgh
Printed and bound in Great Britain by
CPI Antony Rowe, Chippenham and Eastbourne

A CIP record for this book is available
from the British Library

ISBN 0 7486 0467 7

CONTENTS

LIST OF FIGURES AND TABLES

LIST OF ABBREVIATIONS

ACP	African, Caribbean, Pacific
BLDC	Botswana Livestock Development Corporation
BSA Co.	British South Africa Company
BMC	Botswana Meat Commission
CDC	Commonwealth Development Corporation
EC	European Community
FAP	Financial Assistance Policy
HIES	Household Income and Expenditure Survey
NDB	National Development Bank
SIDA	Swedish International Development Authority
TGLP	Tribal Grazing Land Policy

PREFACE

Throughout the sub-continent of southern Africa and beyond, a major trans-formation is in progress, with the transfer to Africans of freehold farms formerly owned by Europeans. Formerly, European ranchers often operated across the international boundaries of Botswana, Zimbabwe and South Africa. In Botswana and Zimbabwe, Africans as new owners, are in no position to do that, but they still participate in regional relations, affected by conditions of supply and demand in the wider market. New forms of ranching have consequently evolved alongside those still practised by European settlers. Today, as in the past, the various forms of ranching continue to be closely inter-connected with, and at times even parasitic upon, indigenous stock keeping.

Despite its importance for development planning in the southern African region, virtually no in-depth research on freehold ranching had been carried out before this study. This book uses an actor-oriented analytical approach to explore the enterprises of ranching in eastern Botswana. The area includes the Tuli Block and the adjacent communal areas, to which the Tuli Block has always been connected by cattle trade and merchant enterprise. The research focuses on the settler farmers, the majority of whom settled before independence, and on the more recently settled African farmers who are mostly part-time and absentee members of the elite.

This book has two main themes. The first is an historical reconstruction of the major transformations and variations in settler ranching highlighting the differential strategies of settlers in coping with change in colonial and post-colonial government policy, as well as change in economic opportunity due to fluctuations in the market. The second theme concerns local farmers and the transformations which have been, and still are, occurring, as former tribesmen become large-scale capitalists, holding land as a commodity, along with livestock as commercial assets. The transformations epitomise many of the major social changes within a wider field in the nation as a whole.

I acknowledge with deep gratitude, the immense assistance which I received from Dr R. P. Werbner, my Ph.D. supervisor in the University of Manchester from January 1984 to December 1987. Through his tireless and far-reaching efforts, it has become possible for me to produce this book. Dr Werbner, with the assistance of his wife, Dr Pninah Werbner, directed with great patience and dedication my earlier work upon which this one is based. I have continued to receive his assistance and support even after completing my Ph.D. It is to him that this book owes its existence. And I remain truly grateful to his whole family for their generosity and kindness towards me both during my study period and after. Nothing I have experienced before matches their concern for me.

A number of prominent scholars have also contributed to my understanding of the issues I confront in this study, among them Dr P. T. W. Baxter, also of the University of Manchester. I am particularly grateful to Dr Ornulf Gulbrandsen of the University of Bergen, for the insight into problems of family labour in the cattle production industry within Botswana's communal areas.

In Botswana, I am indebted to Professor A. K. Datta, the Director of the National Institute for Development Research and Documentation within the University of Botswana, for his constructive criticism of my earlier drafts, and for his general encouragement. I am equally grateful to the University of Botswana for granting me the permission and financial support to carry out further field work in the Tuli Block, and the six month sabbatical during which I have put this study together. My informants, who included highly placed members of the government, notables within the Botswana society and ordinary farmers, gave freely of their knowledge and were kind to me. I thank them all and look to them for further cooperation in the future.

The final edition of this book has been produced under the supervision of Professor Norman Long in the pleasant academic atmosphere of the Department of Rural Sociology of The Tropics, Agricultural University of Wageningen in the Netherlands. I thank Professor Long and the University of Wageningen for that opportunity and privilege.

Finally, I express thanks to the four bodies that have provided financial support for this study. The University of Botswana funded my field work and also paid for my passage to the Netherlands. Living expenses during my sabbatical were covered by a generous grant from the Wenner Gren Anthropological Foundation in the United States. I also received a short fellowship from the Africa Studies Centre, University of Leiden, through the assistance of my friend Professor Wim van Binsbergen. I am grateful to Professor van Binsbergen and to all of these institutions for the financial support they have made available to me.

NOTES ON TEXT

Throughout this study, real names are used for places, but, to protect the anonymity of individuals, pseudonyms are used for all people.

Botswana currency is reckoned in pula, abbreviated to 'P'. During my field work and up to the time of producing this book, the exchange rate was three pula to one pound sterling, and one pula to one Dutch guilder.

1

INTRODUCTION

OBJECTIVE AND SCOPE OF THE STUDY

This is a study of the development of ranching and economic enterprise in the Tuli Block and its adjacent hinterland in eastern Botswana. Although it covers the full range of types of ranching in the Tuli Block as a commercial area, it is not meant to present a comprehensive picture of the entire social transformation. The object is rather to illuminate some of the principal ways in which the different farmers, namely the Afrikaners, the English and the Africans, have continuously transformed their farming enterprises, and the impact this transformation has had on the communities that are part of the ranching systems. Social organisation and its transformation, rather than the economic management of farm units is the focus: how the farmers redirect their entrepreneurship in order to manage changes in economic opportunities and to respond to shifts in the wider political economy, from the colonial period and the arrival of the Europeans in the Tuli Block, to the present and more recent inclusion of Africans as commercial farmers. In the case of the Europeans, the study begins from the colonial period when these farmers settled in the Tuli Block.

Botswana is regarded as a paragon of multi-party based economic development in southern Africa. From a per capita income of US$17 at independence in 1966, the country's economy has grown to an amazing US$1,500 per capita in 1991. Nevertheless, the distribution of income remains skewed, with few people benefiting from this growth. In 1989 the Household Incomes and Expenditure Survey[1] calculated a Gini coefficient of 0.56 as compared with Zambia (0.52). In 1974, Botswana's Gini coefficient was 0.52. It was estimated in 1983 that 53.6 per cent of all rural households were below the poverty datum line. By the year 1990 the percentage of people living under the poverty datum line had risen to a staggering 69 per cent (Botswana Government, 1990). These data mean that despite Botswana's so-called 'miracle story of economic development', poverty and income distribution continue to pose a real problem within the country.

A major issue of this study is to show how differential elite formation has occurred in Botswana. This is an important issue in view of the extraordinary development of Botswana's political economy, as seen in a Third World context. As in most developing countries, only a minority of Batswana are able to reap the benefits of the new economic opportunities and wealth accumulation in terms of state financial resources. This study sets out to show how those who achieve some degree of success actually exploit these opportunities, and analyses how the interface between the characteristics of the different categories of entrepreneurs and the distribution of opportunities produces different types of elite career.

The entry of these emergent African elites into ranching entrepreneurship falls into two broad categories: the national and the district. A simple proposition is that elite entrepreneurship varies with the kind and rank of the African elites. An objective of this study is to describe and analyse different types of entrepreneurs in such a way that variations can be substantiated in depth. Attention is given to the worlds within which both kinds of entrepreneur operate; on the knowledge systems that they put to use in the course of their entrepreneurship; and on how they pool their resources in their struggles with the state and its intermediate structures, as well as their interactions within the communal areas where their enterprises are based.

Two points need to be made. First, concerning the local ranchers only, these entrepreneurs have lifestyles more clearly portrayed through economic activities other than ranching. Primarily they are traders and bureaucrats, and only secondarily ranchers. It is for this reason that in Chapter 4, time is devoted to the analysis of their non-ranching economic activities. The contrary is the case with settler ranchers, for whom the ranch is the springboard for other economic activities, and here more time is devoted to the discussion of their ranching activities.

Second, and not unrelated to the first, concerns the suggestion of land tenure. For both the settler and the local ranchers, Tuli Block ranching spans the freehold farms and the communal areas. Land tenure is different in freehold farms from that of the communal areas. For the purposes of this study, it is not necessary to give a detailed account of the various land tenure arrangements that exist in Botswana. It is sufficient merely to highlight the salient differences between land tenure in the communal areas and on freehold farms.

In the communal areas, land is held by the chief on behalf of the tribe. Grazing pastures are free for all members of the tribe to use. This is particularly the case where natural water resources, such as rivers, are available for the use of livestock producers. Only in the far western part of Botswana, where surface water sources do not exist, is access to the communal range restricted to those livestock producers with boreholes. Such land tenure, where all livestock producers within a tribe have access to pasture, is widely believed

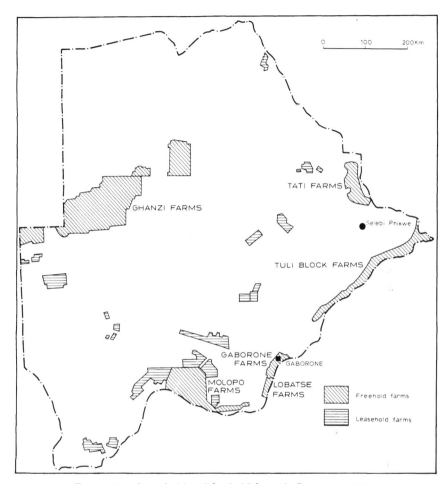

FIGURE 1.1: Leasehold and freehold farms in Botswana, 1980.
Source: Department of Surveys and Lands.

to be the precursor to the 'tragedy of the commons', a situation whereby the range is destroyed through overstocking as every farmer maximises its use. Freehold farms are individually owned property, whose owners do not compete with anyone else for the resources of the farm, including grazing. They can therefore plan the use of their resources optimally, whereas livestock producers in the communal areas are not in a position to do so. On the other hand, cattle production is relatively cheap in the communal areas compared with that on freehold farms.

THE NEED FOR RESEARCH ON RANCHING

With independence in many African countries came increasingly intensified efforts by national and international development agencies to foster commercial ranching. In some of these countries, such as Botswana, Kenya and the Upper Volta, a major goal has been to acquire much-needed foreign currency and state revenue by increasing foreign meat sales. A second announced goal has been ecological: to conserve the range for future generations. It has become conventional wisdom, often repeated in the expert opinions of consultancy reports to governments, that the range has been fast deteriorating under traditional modes of livestock production. Hence, turning pastoralists into beef producers oriented to the market has seemed to be a solution to both economic and ecological problems.

The intensified development of ranching has, of course, not simply been a matter of response to pressures arising from outside the country. The emergence of African elites has contributed to the growth of ranching, and the converse is also true. Ranches, once almost exclusively owned by Europeans, have become much sought prizes to be won by a relatively small African elite as part of their differentiation from the rest of society. It is within this context that the Tribal Grazing Land Policy (TGLP) of 1975 can now be considered. Through the TGLP, the stated intention of government was to commercialise livestock production and conserve the range. These aims were to be achieved through delineating farms, in the communal areas, that would be leased to individuals for up to fifty years. Scholars in general viewed this move as a ploy by the bureaucratic elite to afford themselves, and other cattle magnates, the opportunity not only to have exclusive rights to pastures in the communal areas, but also to own farms. Thus they could separate themselves not only from other cattle owners but also from other members of their community at large.

Even while the TGLP was being implemented, its glaring shortcomings manifested themselves. These included, particularly, the lack of sufficient land on which to delineate the farms and the reluctance of farmers to practise animal husbandry consonant with conventional ranching. Farmers overstocked their farms, and it immediately became evident that the creation of TGLP farms would not achieve range conservation. It remained doubtful too whether the acquisition of the farms by livestock owners who still cherished the idea of being cattle magnates would in any way increase offtake. Planning officers in government have repeatedly called for the scrapping of the TGLP, and, although not accepted by the government, it is a widely held and current view across Botswana that the TGLP has not been a successful policy measure.

The policy measure which undoubtedly has had an impact upon Botswana's ranching industry is the decision by the government to market Botswana's beef to the European Community (EC). In political terms, the joining of the EC market by Botswana in the area of beef is actually a development aid package which is meant to help Botswana's economy through deliberately increased beef prices. However, this move has aggravated ecological problems for Botswana and created difficulties in marketing livestock, putting into relief, in its wider context, the usual contradictions not only in development aid, but in development in general. This is a case where state policy has been conditioned by the interaction between the national economy and the world economy. Facilitation of agribusiness through state-planned intervention aimed at establishing quality controlled beef production for export has become the catalyst for the emergence of contradictory and unintended consequences at the local level, where farmers pay the penalty of the shortcomings of the policy.

Over time, the high-priced EC market precipitates more intensive cattle production beyond the carrying capacity of the range. Moreover, the EC-imposed cordon fences hamper the very ranching in the Tuli Block, for some ranchers disastrously, as exemplified in the profile of a local entrepreneur, Molema, in Chapter 3. Even in the rest of Botswana, Bailey (1982: 51) concludes that the cordon fences have slowed down the pace of cattle movement to markets, with the result that there are now more cattle on the cattleposts than would otherwise have been the case.

A valid counter argument, however, which I fully endorse, is that without the fences Botswana might have been at even greater risk in the event of a disaster such as an outbreak of foot-and-mouth disease, to which the country is so prone. Notwithstanding that, the cost of the cordon fences to the livestock industry has not been recognised.

Currently, countries that constitute Botswana's regular beef market are, in descending order of price: the EC, South Africa, and countries that comprise the 'world market' (see Serema, 1985: 6). Fortunately for Botswana, its two most important markets, the EC and South Africa, are protected through quotas agreed by both trading partners. The EC agreement has been negotiated every five years since 1975, through the Lome Convention; with South Africa, through bilateral arrangements based in part on the understanding and interpretation of the Common Customs Union Agreement of 1910, renegotiated in 1969.

For Botswana and other African, Caribbean and Pacific states (ACP), EC beef prices are almost twice the ruling prices in the world market. The advantage is due, under the Lome Convention, to the exemption from customs duty and from 90 per cent of the variable levy. Botswana's meat sale to South Africa is also tax free.

In Botswana as a whole, especially among the farmers who sell directly to the abattoir, such high beef prices have encouraged more intensive cattle production resulting, in certain areas, in damage to the range (Hitchcock in Picard, 1985: 86–121; Veenendaal and Opschoor, 1986: 24–32, among others). However, access to the EC market is subject to the erection of veterinary cordon fences in Botswana to control foot-and-mouth disease. Strict EC regulations are in force requiring that developing countries construct the cordon fences as a condition for selling their beef to the Community. Botswana, keen to secure a place in this lucrative beef market, has carried out the EC demands to the letter.

The situation in the Tuli Block is worse than the rest of the country, as is already recognised in published form (Bailey, 1982). Cordon fences have restrained cattle marketing throughout Botswana, but the restriction of cattle movement from the Tuli Block to the communal areas, intermittently enforced from 1979 until 1986, has been the greatest setback to post-colonial cattle marketing in the Tuli Block. Like other droughts before it, the 1980–6 drought was followed almost immediately by an outbreak of foot-and-mouth disease. The first step towards control of foot-and-mouth disease has always been to restrict cattle movement. Accordingly, the Tuli Block backline fence was used as a cordon fence. Livestock were not allowed to cross it and leave the Tuli Block. Other lines of cordon fence were also constructed, cutting across the ranches from the backline fence to the river (see Figure 1.2).

Nor is it only the movement of cattle between the Tuli Block and the communal areas that has been hampered by the cordon fences. Also affected has been cattle movement within the Tuli Block. Movement of cattle from one farm to another has always been important for generating quick cash, the basis for the viability of the cattle enterprise on freehold farms. In the period from the establishment of the national abattoir in 1956 to Botswana's independence in 1966, the Tuli Block sustained a considerable but interlinked diversity in the economic activities of farmers. Some ranchers produced immature cattle and sold them to other farmers whose work was to grow them to maturity. These breeds were not the expensive exotic ones but the improved breeds which were cheaper yet still grew fast enough to warrant trade and fattening.

The internal trade within the Tuli Block assured farmers of the quick cash flow which is so crucial, especially for those who relied solely on ranching. Producing and selling immature cattle kept down the costs for both parties. For a single farmer to grow stock to maturity is a long,

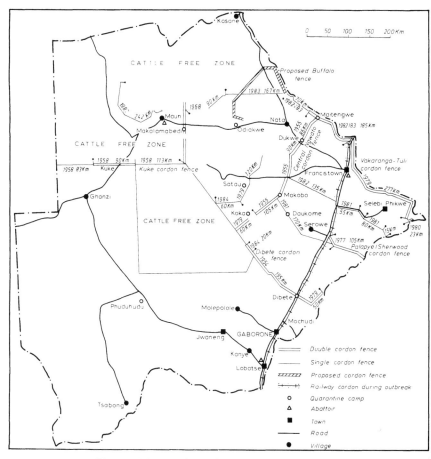

FIGURE 1.2: Veterinary fences in Botswana, 1980.
Source: Department of Veterinary Services.

expensive and risky undertaking. Buyers of immature cattle also had the advantage of realising their cash from sale of mature animals in eighteen to twenty-four months. Buyers and sellers of immature stock therefore, shared the risks of cattle production among them. Buyers also came from the communal areas, mostly under the National Development Bank stocking programme. The erection of the cordon fences across the Tuli Block brought this internal as well as any external trade to a halt.

Construction of cordon fences has set in motion various but related hardships. For many farmers, ranching has ceased to be viable, those without other sources of income being the hardest hit. Within certain ranches, overgrazing has been severely exacerbated.

To conclude, one has to accept that the expansion of Botswana's meat market into the EC has earned the country more foreign exchange than would have been the case if the country had not entered this market. However, less evident is the fact that the demands placed on Botswana by the EC as a condition for buying that meat, have a high ecological cost, which Botswana is already paying. In spite of its positive side, this high cost is now throttling the further development of the cattle industry by cutting back offtake due to the existence of cordon fences.

Such problems, which uncover a whole range of interconnections between elites and policies, indicate that we desperately lack a clear understanding of ranching and the socio-economic issues surrounding it. This book, which is merely a beginning of investigations in this direction, approaches this problem by presenting a comparative analysis of settler and local ranchers in a freehold land setting. The aim, at this point in time, is to understand not so much the technicalities of ranching but the socio-economic processes upon which ranching is based.

HISTORY OF SETTLEMENT AND RANCHING IN THE TULI BLOCK

Ranching in the Tuli Block has a history of unplanned yet highly strategic development, beginning with the arrival of the British South Africa Company (BSA Co.) in Botswana towards the end of the nineteenth century. At that time, the colonial ambitions of the company, and its founder, Cecil Rhodes, were curtailed: the entire country did not actually come under the domination of the company. Instead, in 1895, the Imperial Secretary in Britain responded to lobbying by three of the main tribal chiefs in the country to protect their tribal areas. Eventually, the tribal areas became reserves and other areas, Crown Land. Within the Crown Land, the BSA Co. demarcated European Settlement areas, having been granted a Royal Charter by the Imperial Secretary in 1905 to administer most of the land under European Settlement, including the Tuli Block. An exception was the Tati Concession which was administered by the Tati Company.

The original basis for the BSA Co. claiming the Tuli Block land was that it was needed to construct the railway line across Botswana to the north. However, due mainly to its drainage problems the Tuli Block was found, after survey, to be unsuitable; and the railway line was eventually constructed to the west. No longer needing the land for the railway, Rhodes used it to pursue his imperialist ambitions. He subdivided the area into ranches and settled English-speaking farmers there, in order to encircle the Afrikaners in the Transvaal and to curb their expansion into Botswana.

As early as 1867, some Transvaal farmers, probably Afrikaners, had settled in the Tuli Block, and were using the grazing areas there with the support of the Transvaal government (Coclough and McCarthy, 1980, following Sillery; 1952). However, the BSA Co. was never given freehold title to the three areas it controlled. By contrast, the Tati Company had outright freehold rights to the Tati Concession farms (Croston, 1989: 14). The original intention of the colonial government had been to allow the BSA Co. to grant only occupation certificates to settlers on the blocks that came under its control. In 1903, the British High Commissioner decided to retain the formal right to vet all transfers of title from the company to other parties. The titles were subject to the Bechuanaland Protectorate (Lands) Order-in-Council of 1904, which, inter alia, reserved mineral rights to the Crown.

The transfer of farms by the company to other parties was not without fault. As late as 1953, major discrepancies emerged between the official area of the Tuli Block and the cumulative tally of farm land transferred by the BSA Co. resulting from different methods of surveying the Limpopo river by several surveyors. It appeared that the company had been selling more land than it controlled on paper.

As will be seen below, the entrepreneurs who were the first to buy farms among settlers and even among locals have mostly been those strongly linked to the state. For example, the first farm to be sold in the Tuli Block by the company was bought by a seventy-year-old farmer described as a doyen of the European Advisory Council, and already owning 40,000 hectares (ha.) of farm land in the Gantsi and the Lobatse Blocks.

The pace at which Tuli Block farms were sold gathered momentum with time, beginning somewhat slowly between 1907 and 1911 when only 11 per cent of the Block's farms were sold. By 1950, half of Tuli Block farms had been sold off, totalling 239,464 hectares. Most sales of farms from this European settlement area occurred after World War II. The majority of buyers at this time were Afrikaners from the Transvaal, most of them poor. They moved into the Tuli Block and many took up more isolated farms in the north.

The influx of the Afrikaners after World War II not only illuminates the importance of the connection between the economy of the Tuli Block and that of the Transvaal; it also provides the basis for understanding the change of rules by South Africa pertaining to restrictions on the importation of cattle on the hoof from Botswana. These were applied more rigorously before the advent of the Afrikaners into the Tuli Block and relaxed following their settlement (see below). In addition, the influx shows that the history of Afrikaner settlement in the Tuli Block can be better understood when viewed within the framework of the history of European settlement in South Africa. Grossman (1988) explains that in South Africa land ownership, the prerogative of the nobility in their countries of origin, became possible for every European farmer in the early years of European settlement in that country. From the Cape Colony in the south of the country to the Transvaal in the north each European inhabitant was entitled to apply for unoccupied land to be surveyed and registered in his name. The farmer would pay an annual fee for using the farm (Grossman, 1988: 57). Consequently, virtually all available agricultural land had been occupied by 1930, so that in 1963, only 5.8 per cent of all agricultural land was not privately owned. It seems likely, therefore, that the farmers who moved into neighbouring Tuli Block across the Limpopo were those who had failed to secure land in South Africa, particularly in the Transvaal. Such movement was easy as until Botswana's independence in 1966 the Tuli Block was to all intent and practical purposes treated by the settler farmers as an integral part of the Transvaal.

It is not easy to map the exact sequence of farm sales in the Tuli Block because available documents of farm transfers from one farmer to the next do not always name the buyer; nor do they contain details of purchase price, payment arrangements, dates of transaction, etc.

The interconnection between the Tuli Block and the adjacent farms on the Transvaal side of the Limpopo valley can be further illuminated by the physical connection of some farms on either side of the river, achieved ostensibly for the purpose of making viable the ranching enterprise especially by early Afrikaner settlers. It may have been in response to the need to manage drought risks that some farmers came to have ranches on both sides of the national border formed by the Limpopo river. Oral accounts show that in earlier times when farm boundaries were delineated on the Transvaal side, they were frequently extended to the Botswana side into the Tuli Block. Since such action would not have been in keeping with the intention of Rhodes to circumscribe Afrikaner expansion into the Tuli Block, it is likely that the delineations occcurred before the Tuli Block was given freehold status, or on a few occasions when Afrikaners settled themselves in the Tuli Block without the knowledge and consent of the BSA Co.

The existence of farms spanning the Tuli Block and the Transvaal creates problems in the understanding of simultaneous use of grazing pasture between the two places during colonial times. In some official reports, for instance, there is some ambiguity or disagreement about cross-border cattle movement in the early period. Ranchers are reported to have grazed their cattle freely on either side of the river (Government Report, 1960: 18). Yet in other official reports pertaining to the same period, the rule is understood to have been that cattle movement across the Limpopo river was statutorily forbidden and that this rule was especially enforced during periods of outbreak of cattle lung disease (Government Report, 1954: 16). It is common knowledge among the Tuli Block settlers that as far back as can be recalled, cattle from both sides of the national frontier have drunk from the Limpopo river.

That being so, it is possible that settlers with farms on either side of the river could easily move their herds between their farms. Settlers who have been resident in towns and villages since 1956, recount acts of cattle smuggling, sometimes heavy, from Botswana to South Africa through unauthorised border crossings, especially during the period when South Africa had imposed sanctions on cattle emanating from Botswana. Possibly, many of the cattle were smuggled in the course of being watered since not all of the Limpopo river was guarded by the border police.

Following the world-wide recession of the 1930s, it is important to chronicle events leading to the increased cattle sales to South Africa from the whole of Botswana and not only from the Tuli Block. An account of the changes and adjustments made by farmers to take full advantage of the post-recession boom is important not least because today those farmers that have retained the changes in the organisation of their enterprises have expanded such enterprises, some of them considerably, while those farmers that have not maintained the changes have gone bankrupt, despite the enormous scale that their enterprises had reached in colonial times. Chapter 2 deals with this when the profiles of the settler entrepreneurs are presented.

The period immediately following the years of recession, 1930–3, saw a boom in the South African mining industry, which is based mainly in the Witwatersrand region of the Transvaal. The boom in mining triggered a demand for beef for the mine workers. South Africa, unable to cope with the demand, looked to Botswana for the provision of live cattle that would be slaughtered in the Johannesburg abattoirs. To enable Botswana to supply the required beef to the Transvaal, changes had to be made within the state machinery and within the social organisation of the farmers themselves. Whereas up to this point the state had insisted that settlers did not buy scrab cattle from the communal areas for fattening on their farms – directing instead that settlers should produce high quality beef – the rule was rescinded and settlers were encouraged and assisted to buy cattle from Africans in the communal areas, selling them into South Africa in turn. A measure of such assistance from the state was the monopoly that the settlers had in selling cattle to South Africa, being given licences to deal in cattle while Africans were denied such licences in an effort to keep them from competing with the settlers. Africans could sell cattle only among themselves or to Europeans, but not to South Africa.

The use of trading licences by the colonial government to protect settler interests at the expense of locals was not peculiar to Botswana, but a widely held practice throughout what Amin calls 'the Africa of the labour reserves' (Kennedy, 1988: 11–29). Amin observes that in the Africa of the labour reserves Africans were restricted from entering such trade for two reasons: first to avoid competition with Europeans, and second to encourage emigration of Africans to work in the South African mines. It must be observed, however, that exemptions were occasionally given to chiefs and some members of the African nobility by the colonial administration, ostensibly to strengthen the British colonial system of indirect rule. Such exemptions included permission given to chiefs to sell their cattle to South Africa.

In order to facilitate the purchase of cattle from Africans, the settlers took on a new role; they became traders with stores on or near their farms. It was through such stores that they bought the cattle. During drought years some of them exchanged corn from their stores for cattle from Africans. During the boom period of the mining industry in South Africa, mentioned above, cattle from the communal areas did not stay long on the settler farms. The great demand for their meat in South Africa ensured that they merely passed through the farms where they were held while arrangements were being made to trek or rail them to Johannesburg (subject to restrictions which will be discussed later). Yet, at the same time, settlers also bought cheap immature stock to grow to maturity on their own farms, and took advantage of the market by holding cattle until prices in the Transvaal improved (Croston, 1989: 18).

From the foregoing it can be seen that the influx of the Afrikaner settlers into the Tuli Block after World War II, though partly caused by shortage of land in South Africa, was also partly induced by cattle trade between Botswana and South Africa. Not all settlers became traders, however; at least one account indicates a conflict of interest between trading and non-trading settlers. Without giving a time-frame for the incidents, Croston states that the drive by non-trading farmers to seal off the Tuli Block from the adjacent communal reserve whenever there was an outbreak of disease sparked off major quarrels between the two types of farm holders (Croston, 1989: 18).

It must be stressed that cattle sales did not take place within an international free market. It suited the Transvaal that the importation of cattle from Botswana was controlled and restricted. Ettinger (1972) states that the restriction was not in the form of open quotas; but through controls disguised as regulations on the minimum allowable weight of cattle at the point of entry into South Africa. Between 1939 and 1941, for instance, the Union imposed a minimum weight of 1,000 lbs for oxen and 750 lbs for cows sold at the Johannesburg abattoirs. This was at a time when there was a large enough supply of meat from within South Africa. Farmers from South Africa argued that meat from outside their country had the effect of lowering the price within. Also, the Tuli Block was at this time settled predominantly by English-speaking farmers who were regarded less favourably by the South African community than Afrikaner settlers would have been.

An account of economic developments within a micro study cannot fail to explicate the interconnections between the study area and developments in the rest of the world. Developments within the Tuli Block were as much influenced by outside events as they were by local events. For example, in the 1950s, Britain was short of US dollars and decided to discontinue the importation of meat from the United States, preferring instead to import meat from its colonies. As a result, an export abattoir was opened in Botswana in 1955, following an earlier attempt in the 1930s which failed. The export abattoir had a monopoly to export meat as well as livestock on the hoof, the meat being shipped mainly to Britain, with South Africa occasionally receiving some cattle on the hoof.

The opening of the export abattoir brought about a significant change in the cattle trade between Botswana and South Africa as well as within Botswana itself. Pressured by the atmosphere of political change around the world as colonies attained their independence, the colonial government decided to allow Africans to market their cattle direct to the abattoir, thus effectively removing the protection that the settlers had enjoyed. This resulted in a situation whereby the abattoir found itself without the capacity to process all cattle offered for sale by the farmers.

Settlers on freehold farms stood to lose greatly from these developments, mainly because they could no longer organise the protected cross-border cattle sales upon which their farm business depended. The Tuli Block transformed from being merely a cattle-holding area into one in which cattle were now being produced. But cattle production carried a greater risk and also entailed raising the standard of the farms to conventional levels; it was costlier than cattle-holding which had been achieved with less risk on simpler, less costly farms.

In response to the subsequent loss of profit which was quite substantial for some settlers, many departed the Tuli Block for South Africa while others moved into the villages in Botswana and became merchant traders. This latter move would have been quite easy because for some years following the opening of the abattoir, Europeans still held the monopoly of general licences and were allowed to operate within the communal areas as traders, even though they were not allowed to keep cattleposts. Still others remained in the Tuli Block.

The differential response of the settlers to these changes is comparable to that of settlers on the North American Plains in the eighteenth century. Bennet writes of them:

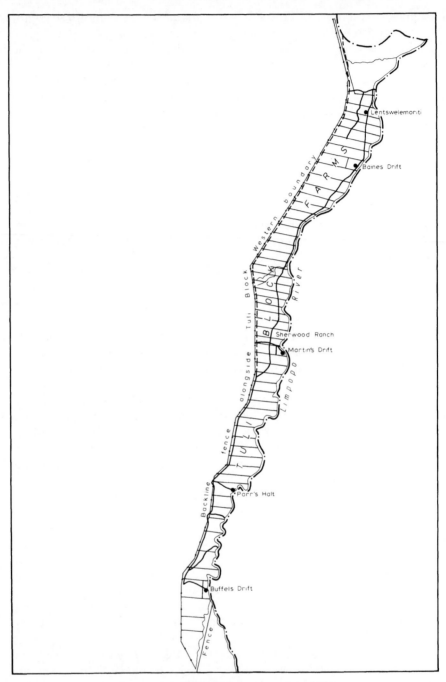

FIGURE 1.3: Tuli Block farms, around 1956.
Source: Department of Surveys and Lands, 1990.

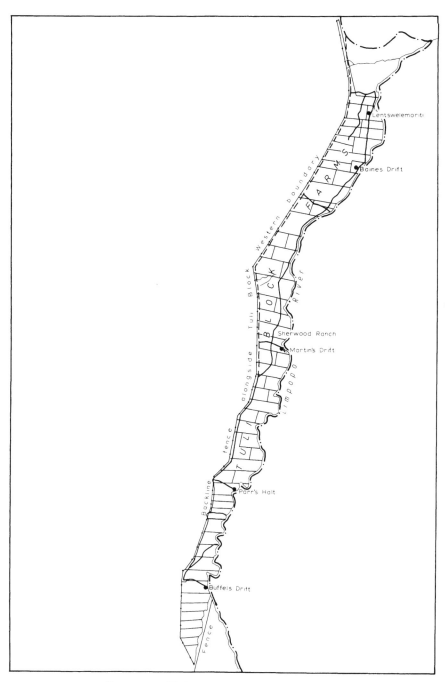

FIGURE 1.4: Tuli Block farms, around 1989.
Source: Department of Surveys and Lands, 1990.

they were cosmopolitan or heterogeneous in terms of their background. Some were land speculators, others wanted to get rich quick on a bumper crop. Many of them left after realising the difficulty of the trade. Some were men who merely wanted to subsist. The depression of 1930 forced out the last of those who lacked the desire, skill, funds, to make a life on the Plains. (Bennett, 1979: 214–15)

In the same way Tuli Block settlers were not a homogeneous group in any sense: they must have differed in terms of their resources and intentions. Such variation in their means and intentions must also have been instrumental in their differential response to the changing entrepreneurial climate. Allowing for that, at independence in 1966, the Tuli Block, though highly prized by Africans, had lost the profitability of its early years, the period between the recession and the opening of the abattoir.

THE TULI BLOCK COMPARED WITH OTHER EUROPEAN SETTLEMENT AREAS

In 1905 the Tuli Block was, of course, only one of the ranching areas given to European farmers by the BSA Co. (see Figure 1.1). The others were Gantsi, Lobatse and Gaborone. The Molopo farms were added later, and in the case of the Tati Concession which was administered by the Tati Company in north-eastern Botswana, part was set aside for a reserve, and part for freehold farms. But in various respects, the Tuli Block was the most important of these settlements. It was and is the largest; stretching for 130 miles along the 770-mile long Botswana-Transvaal border (Stevens, 1969), with an area of 3,900 square miles (Samboma, 1979). Within the Limpopo valley that spans Botswana and the Transvaal, Tuli Block ranches are bounded to the east by the perennial Limpopo river; on no other freehold block is there a perennial river. To the north, the Tuli circle forms the frontier between the Tuli Block and ranches in Zimbabwe. This location of the Tuli Block makes it of considerable strategic importance, economically and politically. Furthermore the Tuli Block is the most developed of the former European settlement areas in terms of the condition of farms, the quality of farmhouses and the roads linking it with the rest of Botswana and also with South Africa. It would seem that, for these very good reasons, the settlers saw the Tuli Block as the jewel in the crown by comparison with other ranching blocks in Botswana. Hence, for the biggest among African cattle owners, it has long been a prize objective particularly once the move towards commercialisation of livestock production in the 1960s and the privatisation of land within the communal areas in the mid-1970s became strong.

RANCHING AND CLASS FORMATION IN POST-COLONIAL BOTSWANA

The commercialisation of livestock production in the 1960s and the privatisation of land within the communal areas in the mid-1970s were not unrelated events. They were reflections of a general trend that was unfolding around the sub-continent at that period. Ranching in post-colonial Botswana must be understood within this context. In Botswana, cattle ownership has continued to be the yardstick of the scale of social influence. A major reason for this is the lack of opportunities for investment outwith the cattle industry. The national economy, based on minerals, especially diamonds, has grown rapidly at an average of 12 per cent per annum since independence. Faced with lack of opportunities to invest in other sectors of the economy, those who have benefited from this growth have invested in cattle.

Investment in cattle has occurred for both economic and social reasons and ranch ownership has been viewed largely as a sign of success in large-scale ranching and a consolidation of the ranching enterprise. Ranch ownership has come to be taken as a mechanism for measuring social differentiation among cattle producers. Ranch-based social differentiation has occurred at two unequal levels, the district and the national. It is for this reason that I make reference to the district elite as well as the national. The differentiation has to do with the geographical sphere of influence. The influence of district elites is limited to the districts where such elites live, while that of the national elite is countrywide. Further explanation on these terms is given below.

Drought has been a very significant factor in the post-colonial ranching enterprise. The expansion of cattle grazing into the formerly unentered pastures of western Botswana was prompted partly by lack of grazing in the more densely inhabited eastern part of the country. The twenty-year drought period which spanned the 1960s to the 1980s gave further opportunity for economic differentiation in cattle enterprise. Farmers with means penetrated the wild west where they sank boreholes and established cattleposts around which they had exclusive pastures. Though the west is partly a semi-desert without surface water sources, it has large quantities of potential grazing pastures. When the drought struck, the larger cattle owners took advantage of the abundant pastures of western Botswana where their cattle could graze without competition from other people's herds. In due course, a number of such farmers have been able to raise substantial herds in this manner.

The framing of the TGLP to which reference was made earlier, and the delineation of the Nojane farms which will be discussed later, took place within the framework of the need for exclusive use of pastures by the larger farmers, as did the purchase of farms by locals on freehold land like the Tuli Block and other blocks. A host of different but related factors such as commercialisation of beef production, privatisation of communal land, ownership of freehold land, economic expansion of individuals and social differentiation among cattle producers affected the outcome. It is no wonder, therefore, that local farmers have gone into commercial beef production without any

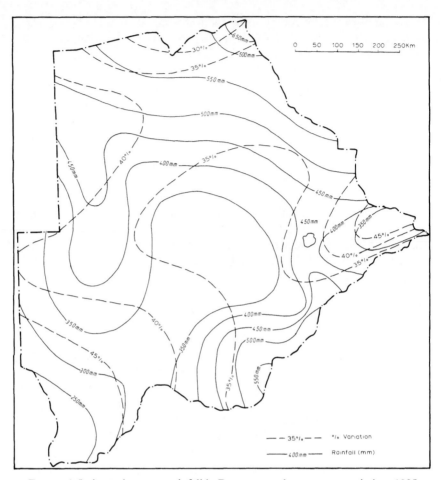

FIGURE 1.5: Annual average rainfall in Botswana and percentage variation, 1985.
Source: Department of Meteorological Services.

experience in conventional ranching, as will be seen from the cases described later.

The strong association between government policy and large-scale ranching in post-colonial Botswana is quite conspicuous: large-scale ranchers in the post-colonial era have depended upon the state for their business and the state has subsidised the cattle industry. The case of the TGLP and that of the Nojane farms show that it is the large-scale farmers who have enjoyed the heaviest subsidies and privileges. Only the large-scale farmers qualified for a ranch in either case. Some farmers obtained more than one ranch. This point leads us to an important feature of the livestock development policy in the post-colonial era around the sub-region. In general, cattle barons have influenced the livestock development policy in their favour. (Cheater confirms this for Zimbabwe (1984).) In Botswana, this has been made easier by the fact that the top policy makers at the national level are cattle barons. Hence, loans were procured from the World Bank and the Swedish International Development Authority (SIDA) with the approval of the Botswana Parliament to finance the establishment of TGLP and Nojane farms.

However, while the social context within which the local farmers obtained freehold and other types of farms was the same, the manner in which the different types of farms were acquired varied widely and this is also true of the way freehold farms are being used vis-à-vis TGLP farms. Freehold farms were bought without any state subsidy, whereas TGLP farms were leased freely to farmers. Some freehold farms have basic conventional ranching requisites like fencing, water sources and paddocks. These requisites enable the new farm owners to carry out certain higher order livestock production procedures, like controlled breeding, which are difficult to carry out on the TGLP farms because these are undeveloped. Partly for this reason, a freehold farm purchased from the settlers is widely regarded as a far greater asset than a TGLP farm, which is used mainly as an exclusive cattlepost.

One of the differences, therefore, between a TGLP and a freehold farm is the state subsidy. Local farmers who failed to pay for their freehold farms lost the farms to their creditors. Most local farmers used a National Development Bank loan to buy their freehold farms. The repossession of the farms by this bank, which is a government institution, signified that the state saw a difference between a TGLP and a freehold farm. It would appear that the view of the state is that a freehold farm is a privilege and the preserve of the most successful rancher. Since its ownership is a clear social differentiation mechanism among ranchers, the state might be right in insisting that no government subsidy be given for the acquisition of this kind of farm by an individual.

That notwithstanding, the general context within which all kinds of farms were acquired in the post-colonial era remains the same. Also, in the post-colonial era as in the colonial, ranching has depended very much upon the

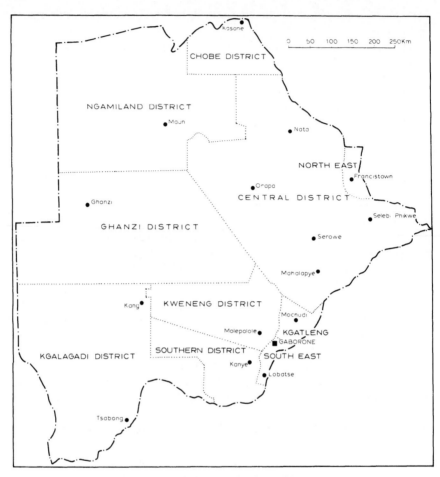

FIGURE 1.6: Botswana districts, 1990.
Source: Department of Surveys and Lands.

link between a farm and the cattlepost. The case material in this book shows that the evolution of the new elite, like the continuation and sustenance of the old, took place on the back of state-subsidised ranching which spanned the commercial and the communal areas.

SUMMARY OVERVIEW

This book is divided into five chapters, Chapter 1 being the introduction. In Chapter 2, profiles of settler entrepreneurs are presented. The chapter opens with a brief introduction to the profiles. More time is spent on the alternative settler firms of Vorster, the paternalist entrepreneur who develops a familist strategy in the organisation and management of his family firm, and Charles, the technocratic entrepreneur who develops an individualist strategy. Profiles of other settlers are given only a brief treatment, the aim being to highlight more variation as well as to allow for the emergence of general trends in settler mediation.

Chapter 3 provides an in-depth analysis of the different factors in settler mediation as stipulated in the case material. Central to the analysis is the dependence of the familist firm on social resources and the dependence of the individualist firm on state resources. The overall strategies of the two firms: the choice of technocratic mediation, specialisation in exotic breeds, and individualism for the English firm; and paternalism, multiple enterprise, the use of local community resources, and familism for the Afrikaner firm, are predicated jointly by this difference as well as by the labour situation within the two families.

In Chapter 4, the focus of the study shifts from the settlers to the locals. The chapter is a documentation of brief profiles of five local entrepreneurs: Pule, a member of the national elite; Tau, Molema and Kgari, three members of the district elite; and, Pitso, a non-elite. The brevity of the profiles is a reflection of the short history of freehold ranching among locals. Unlike the profiles of the alternative settler entrepreneurs which contain the history of ranching in the Tuli Block, the profiles of the local entrepreneurs lack this useful historical dimension which illuminates the context within which their ranching occurs.

To make up for this shortfall, I prepare the ground for the profiles by providing background information to the transition of local ranching from the communal areas to freehold farms. The background information stresses the need to view the transition from communal areas to farms as part and parcel of the state formation process in the post-colonial era, and also as something that is taking place all over the developing world. I emphasise that the elite perceive this development more clearly than do the non-elite, hence the differences between the two groups in the reasons for purchasing a ranch. The differences in the reasons for buying a farm are, of course, not limited to this perception.

In Chapter 5, the conclusion, I look back at the whole study and bring into sharper focus what I consider to be the underlying patterns in the interface issues and the differential response of the entrepreneurs to change. For purposes of exposition, I present the different aspects of the underlying patterns, in turn, stressing that the aspects, like the associated patterns as a whole, are interrelated. In this regard, I re-focus on bordermanship, multiple enterprise vis-à-vis specialisation, the role of the state, the dynamics of labour, and social networks.

Throughout the study, the terms 'farm' and 'ranch' are used interchangeably. A related term that is used frequently, but one that is not quite interchangeable with these two above, is 'firm'. This term encompasses the entire enterprise of a farmer. It includes non-farm operations which, as we have shown, are for some farmers more important than the agribusiness.

NOTE

1. The Household Incomes and Expenditure Survey (HIES) is an economic data collection exercise carried out annually by the Ministry of Finance and Developing Planning for the purpose of mapping economic changes among households in all of the major settlements in Botswana.

2

PROFILES OF SETTLER ENTREPRENEURS

This chapter concentrates on two case studies of settler ranching. Each case is a micro-history of change in a family firm over at least three generations, and culminates in the emergence of two extreme types, the paternalist entrepreneur and the technocrat. Because they represent extremes of development, I refer to them as alternative settler firms. My primary concern here is to describe the cases in depth and thus to provide the analysis with a substantial empirical basis. Two other short profiles of settler firms are presented for the sake of highlighting a broader spectrum of variation in settler enterprise. The diversity in styles of farming as captured in these four settler cases, as well as the cases of the local entrepreneurs described in Chapter 4, reveal the complexity of the interrelationships of the units and elements of ranching. However, the major focus is on the cases of the alternative settlers because they each contain a long micro-history of change.

A central theme of the cases of the alternative settler entrepreneurs is expansion under a changing political economy. Members of each ranch try in their different ways to find and keep a niche for themselves within the successive political economies. In the main, they do so by seizing upon the market opportunities that are created by the state – directly in the case of the individualist firm, and indirectly in the case of the alternative familist firm. The first half of each profile is about change under the management of the oldest living generation; in the second half, the focus is on developments introduced by a younger member of the family ranch.

VORSTER, THE PATERNALIST ENTREPRENEUR

This case highlights the division of labour within the family and the diversification of members' contributions to family enterprise. Much attention is paid to the importance of clientage or paternalist entrepreneurship, and a kinship ideology – an ideology of incorporating the firm within the family. Clientage and kinship are combined to bring about a positive force in the expansion of commercial entrepreneurship. The focus in Phase one, below, is on the present head of the family, Vorster. Phase two focuses on Verlem, his eldest son.

Phase one

Vorster, an Afrikaner now in his mid-seventies, came, roughly in 1934, from the Transvaal. His father bought a 4,280-ha. Tuli Block farm, having sold the family's small Transvaal farm with its main crop of groundnuts. In his twenties, Vorster was sent to a village thirty-five miles away in the communal areas to work for an Afrikaner trader. Vorster's younger brother remained on their Tuli Block farm growing groundnuts. I have little information about Vorster's younger brother. Relations between him and Vorster appear to be extremely bad. Neither Vorster nor his children like to talk about him. He recently sold his farm at the southern end of Vorster's but to some other man, and remains on a part of it as the owner of a small store.

At the beginning, times were hard, Vorster remembers. In South Africa, they had been poor farmers, marketing their groundnuts through the Cooperative in Potgietesrus. They owned basic implements only, such as the ox-drawn plough and the harrow. Their African labour was hired from the nearby villages. In the Tuli Block, although the Limpopo river, the international boundary and the farm's eastern limit, had abundant water after the drought, they practised dryland farming. The machinery needed for irrigation was too costly for them. In the Transvaal, the main source of credit was the Land Bank and it was not always easy for it to extend credit to farmers who were in Botswana following the Union of South Africa's failure to incorporate it.

External credit was, however, of great importance for this family firm's development. No sooner had Vorster settled in the village than the great cattle trade between Botswana and the Transvaal began, after the end of the 1929–34 depression. Capital for cattle trading was controlled by Johannesburg livestock agents (see Hubbard, 1983: 12–14). They extended it into Botswana through carefully selected settler farmers who could be used to buy cattle from the communal areas. Vorster's father was one of these credit-worthy settlers; he found favour with the livestock agents and consequently switched over to cattle buying, starting as an agent. After realising that more cattle-holding ground was needed to avoid overgrazing, the cattle traders advanced Vorster's father the money to buy a farm measuring 216 ha. in 1938.

There was a general pattern among white settlers in the cattle trade at this time. Initially, cattle were bought at kraal auctions or at settler owned stores in villages. Later on, stores on some farms were also introduced. The cattle were either trekked immediately to Johannesburg or kept at first on the farms, awaiting trekking. Officially, the cattle were allowed to cross only at the border post manned by veterinary personnel and equipped with weighing bridges. There were only two such border posts; one at the southern tip of the Tuli Block in Sikwane, and the other one further south at Ramatlabama in the southern part of Botswana.

Within five years of the start of this trade, the abundance of externally provided cash and the readily available cattle from Botswana flooded the Transvaal cattle markets. In order to protect its cattle farmers from the low prices which resulted from a flooded market, the South African government subverted the terms of the regional customs union agreement. Contrary to the aims of the customs union, the South African government introduced and enforced in 1939, sanctions in cattle trade from Botswana, Lesotho and Swaziland (Peters, 1985: 109). Probably due to uncertainty about the future trading relations between Botswana and South Africa, the livestock agents were, this time, reluctant to solve the problem of insufficient cattle-holding land by extending credit to the Tuli Block farmers. The effects of sanctions in cattle dealing were felt most by farmers with many cattle. Among these farmers was Vorster's father. Nevertheless, he bought a 5,000-ha. ranch in 1940; and did so without the assistance of creditors. Vorster himself had been conscripted into the army to fight in the Second World War a year earlier.

The period of restricted cattle trade from 1939 to 1941 was characterised by heavy cattle smuggling from Botswana to the Transvaal. In Botswana, settler cattle agents and farmers, and the wealthier among local Africans were involved (Ettinger, 1972: 24; Peters, 1985: 109–12). Peters in particular, states that those participating most actively were the settlers and local Africans who had relatives in South Africa. Among the settlers, the Afrikaners, more commonly than the English, had homes in the Transvaal. Apparently, Vorster's father was heavily involved in cattle smuggling. At least this is the view of some settler ranchers currently in the Tuli Block, and others in other freehold areas, as well as some elderly villagers living adjacent to Vorster's farm. Vorster's father is said to have crossed cattle across the Limpopo river opposite his farms at night and to have sent them initially to his small Potgietesrus farm. From there, it is said, the cattle would be trekked to the Johannesburg markets.

When the sanctions were lifted in 1941, Vorster's father was already fully established on his own, no longer working for his former creditors. Their relations had soured when the creditors pressed for the repayment of the outstanding loan. Upon Vorster's return from the army in 1945, his father cleared the outstanding balance on the loan with the creditors, possibly with money raised by Vorster through his army service. In addition to this enhancement of its credit-worthiness, the family firm diversified its interests by building a hotel on their farm near the Limpopo river and a border post. Apparently, the immediate aim was to occupy Vorster's mother as its manager; at that time she had been relatively idle. As Benedict says, family firms sometimes venture into new enterprises in order to occupy idle family hands (Benedict, 1968: 11–13). The hotel's patrons, at least in the public bar and restaurant, were mostly the ranchers from both sides of the frontier. The family sold the hotel in 1962, once it was evident that easy traffic across the frontier was to end. The border fence was constructed on the Transvaal side of the frontier, and Botswana's independence was imminent.

The commercial training that Vorster gained under the Afrikaner trader was the beginning of his career as a large merchant trader. At the death of the Afrikaner trader in 1949, Vorster's father bought the trader's store. Two years later, Vorster's father himself died. That year also, Vorster married a relative of his mother's whose natal home was in South Africa. Over the decades after his return from the war, Vorster established himself as a patron with a circle of protégés and clients, both African and Afrikaner, tied to him in various ways. Short of family labour following his father's death, Vorster trained some carefully selected African protégés to manage his shops and to link him with other Africans. These African protégés, as I show below, have facilitated Vorster's cattle-buying at auctions. Vorster was also able to forge strong and lasting links with some Afrikaners in the Tuli Block. For instance, he helped settle a newly arrived Afrikaner from the Transvaal by initially employing him as a cattle-buying agent. After a few years, the two men bought a ranch jointly, then sold it after a year and shared the money. In turn, this Afrikaner bought a ranch on his own account. Eventually, he married Vorster's daughter (see Baxter, 1985, about similar practices among a totally different ethnic group, the Borana stock owners in Kenya). His ranch is within the vicinity of Vorster's ranches as is the ranch of Vorster's other affine, the Afrikaner father of the wife of his eldest son.

On nearby ranches, Vorster has surrounded himself with less prosperous business allies, virtually his clients who are also his affines. As their patron, he helps his neighbours by lending them his cattle-buying licences and also sells them treated timber poles for ranch fences. However, the relationship with neighbours as clients has a commercial basis: the neighbours pay where they must, although the terms of payment are deliberately made lenient. The basic idiom of the neighbourhood set is that economic production must be at the centre of all activities. Because of commoditisation, market relations become dominant as social relations of production.

In terms of social organisation, Vorster has developed a commercial network for cattle purchasing in the communal areas that is important for distinguishing him from other ranchers. He buys cattle on all three auction days of the week, Monday, Tuesday and Fridays in the villages around his ranches. Each of the three villages has only one day a week to auction cattle. That gives him the chance to attend all three auctions. If he cannot attend, his eldest son attends on his behalf. His African protégés do not miss such auctions. They negotiate prices on Vorster's behalf among their fellow Africans before the auction begins. During the auction, these protégés merely support Vorster's bids. In return for their services, Vorster ploughs their arable fields for substantially reduced charges and also employs their children at slightly higher wages than usual. This symbiotic relationship reinforces the philosophy of clientage between Vorster and his protégés.

In 1954, Botswana's own abattoir was opened in Lobatse, bringing to an end the live cattle sales by individuals across the border, especially to South Africa. Cattle from Botswana, especially from south-eastern Botswana, of which the Tuli Block is a part, had to be sold to the abattoir. However, the abattoir was unable to kill all cattle offered for sale. This was so because of the abattoir's small size, and the pressure was too great, despite the reduction in the volume of trade occasioned by the withdrawal of the Johannesburg livestock agents in the months preceding its opening. Income from ranching dropped and ranches held livestock for longer than before.

In order to cope with the post-1954 changes in the cattle industry, Vorster devoted much of his time to trading in consumer goods and agricultural equipment. At present he buys merchandise from his home town of Potgietesrus in the Transvaal where he is reported to own a wholesale outlet, a farm and a two-storeyed house. (In the region, a two-storeyed house denotes success in entrepreneurship.) The consumer goods are then distributed through Vorster's wholesale-cum-retail outlet on his farm. Delivered to his stores in the nearby villages, they are retailed for cash and also bartered for cattle and goats.

A milestone in the expansion of Vorster's business was his purchase in 1984 of a farm in the Transvaal, opposite his Tuli Block farm. I am not sure of its size, nor do I have any certain information on the reason why it was bought. Its location is, of course, strategic and other settler, as well as local, ranchers suspect that it aids smuggling; Vorster himself has the reputation of being a cattle smuggler in the Tuli Block. As demonstrated later in this chapter through the citation of a court case, he has been caught in the act of smuggling hides and skins of cattle and wildlife across the frontier.

In terms of overall business strategy, Vorster is a multiple entrepreneur. With particular reference to ranching, he has purposely chosen not to be a specialist breeder of exotic breeds. He has made his choice despite recognising the high social and economic values of exotic breeds. His breeding of improved bulls with trade cows is very limited. He prefers, instead, to rely more heavily on speculation or grazing. His ownership of 40,000 ha. of land in 1990 makes him one of the largest ranchers in the northern Tuli Block. The size of his ranch also allows him enough land to stock and fatten great numbers of cattle traded from the communal areas. Vorster barters ox ploughs, donkey carts and other machinery which form part of his merchandise, in exchange for cattle and goats. An ox plough costing £20 is bartered in exchange for one beast, while a donkey cart that cost £167 is exchanged for six beasts. These prices vary slightly according to the economic relationship between Vorster and the other party. In this way, then, he is able to link ranching with retail trade based upon his wholesale enterprise.

Upon sale of stock at the abattoir, Vorster gets an average of £250 per beast. This means a considerable profit. The sum is usually for cattle bought originally from the communal areas for about £130. It is a profit margin of almost 100 per cent, despite the real costs incurred in growing the beast to full maturity.

Not that cattle producers in the communal areas price their cattle low: rather, like all speculators, Vorster drives a hard bargain. To appreciate his superior position relative to theirs in this and other matters, Vorster's role as a paternalist entrepreneur has to be considered further. Of particular importance here is the trade from clients. Vorster buys cattle and goats from as many people as possible. Nevertheless, a substantial number are his customers or clients in the merchant trade. As such, they curry favour and do not wish to lose their connection with him. They are well aware that if disaster such as drought strikes, their survival depends very much on the kind of relationship they have with him. Or rather, that is how they have come to perceive their situation. This perception makes Vorster's clients accept whatever reasonable price he offers, although, as is shown later, they devise various means to counter the losses they incur through this relationship. This subordination of their immediate economic interests is apparently made easier by barter which marks a distortion in the conversion and goes some way to equating values.

Vorster markets his cattle to the abattoir by an entrepreneurial method that maximises his returns and minimises his reliance upon outsiders, other than his own family. His system gives him an edge over many other northern Tuli Block ranchers. Once the annual Botswana Meat Commission (BMC) cattle purchase calendar is made public, it shows the months of sale for all areas in the country. With this information, Vorster plans his quota applications. Vorster and his sons have individual cattle buying permits and are thus entitled as registered producers, to sell cattle directly to the BMC. All of them apply for quotas so that their requests are enough for the needs of the ranch as a whole. More often than not, in the applications the requests are inflated above the actual herd for sale. This practice, common among large cattle producers and speculators throughout the country, is in response to abattoir policy. The abattoir reduces the quota per applicant if the total number of cattle offered for sale exceeds the abattoir's slaughtering capacity. Vorster's entrepreneurial method of marketing is not merely a matter of family cooperation, however; liquidity is also maximised in Vorster's method. He is the only rancher who consistently uses his own vehicles to transport his cattle to the abattoir, some 220 miles away. Apart from Vorster and one parastatal ranch, other ranchers trek their cattle to the railhead and have them freighted to the abattoir by rail. At the BMC abattoir in Lobatse, Vorster personally supervises the transaction. He does not use agents, because they would charge him commission per animal sold. Moreover, he sees his cattle across the killing floor in order to make sure that the abattoir staff do not interchange his and other people's cattle, as it were, by mistake. On the following day he is able to return to the Tuli Block with his money in his pocket, unlike the many Tuli Block farmers who use cattle agencies. Such farmers may wait up to twenty-one days for their cheques. Vorster's marketing method thus has a considerable advantage in liquidity. As a speculator, he needs ready cash all the time. In his choice of direct marketing to the abattoir he has had that in mind.

I now turn to the kinship ideology which is the engine that drives Vorster's enterprise. The nature of Vorster's enterprise at this phase is an outgrowth of an Afrikaner familist tradition, which owes much to a peasant history (on Afrikaner farming in the nineteenth century, see Wellington, 1932; Russell and Russell, 1979). Vorster runs this family enterprise as a whole with his sons. I know of no other Afrikaner farmer in the Tuli Block who has managed such family unity. Vorster's enterprise is undivided in terms of profit sharing according to fixed shares for family members. Wages are not paid to Vorster's sons. They merely draw according to their needs. The joint arrangement of the firm assures them of a high standard of living, reflective of the success of the enterprise, even giving them free use of expensive cars bought and maintained by the enterprise.

Vorster himself seems to have learned a lesson from his experience with his own brother, making him aware of the conflicts which may arise in the process of partitioning inheritance. Hence, Vorster has already laid down guidelines and a sound basis for the partitioning of his and his wife's estate upon inheritance by his sons. Each of the first two sons has a house in his own part of the ranching estate. The last unmarried son, who completed his schooling in 1986, is named after his father, and lives with him in the main house. In different parts of the hinterland covered by Vorster's merchant trading, each of the three sons co-manages a store with Vorster. The last son co-manages the store on the ranch; the middle son the one in the nearest village, and the eldest son the store in the farthest village from the ranch. This physical separation of their trading concerns is meant to obviate conflict that could arise from competition between them.

It would appear that in co-managing his stores with his sons, Vorster deliberately intends that his sons appreciate the need to continue to link ranching with merchant trading. After he and his wife have died, the ranch is to be shared in three equal parts by his sons, the youngest occupying the main house. The stores are to be shared according to the existing pattern of co-management. Vorster's sons say that their sister was given her share of inheritance when she married. This, they say, is 'the Afrikaner way' of inheritance. A cross-checking of the validity of this statement across the border in the Transvaal suggested that this is no longer common practice, although it was perhaps an ideal some time ago. In part, the change is due to the fact that South African law prohibits the partitioning of ranching land beyond a certain minimum size.

I am not sure what would happen if Vorster's wife survived him. Perhaps the enterprise would be run somewhat as it is now. In family firms elsewhere, during the survival of one parent, division is often postponed (see Long, 1974). It remains to be seen whether the property will be divided according to plan in the event of both parents dying.

So far, I have viewed the firm in terms of protégés and family members in management. I now consider the rest of the workforce. The regular workforce of thirty-six in Vorster's enterprise is exceptionally large by contemporary Tuli Block standards. The hired labour force is divided unevenly between the three units which bring most of the cash-flow into the enterprise; eight in merchant trading, where they serve mostly as store assistants, twelve in the livestock unit, where they are engaged mainly as herders, and two tractor drivers in the arable production unit. Of the units which are mainly for providing services, the most heavily capitalised is transport. This unit is essentially concerned with hauling merchandise from South Africa via the Tuli Block to stores in the villages, and transporting cattle to the abattoir. The two truck drivers drive two articulated trucks with a cargo carrying capacity of 20 tonnes each. Fence repairing with its small timber treatment plant maintained by eight employees, constitutes the second main service unit. The firm orders plain timber poles from South Africa, which are then treated with tar and then used to repair the perimeter fence. Any excess is sold to Vorster's affines within his neighbourhood set.

Finally, within the service unit are the domestic staff; in the main ranch house a cook, a house-cleaner, a washerwoman and a courtyard cleaner. Each of the two houses occupied by Vorster's sons has a female domestic servant who does all the housework by herself. Each is able to accomplish this task because each house is much smaller than that of Vorster's.

Nor are these the only workers in this enterprise. On a property that has some 4,000 ha. under cultivation, seasonal labour is needed for the main crop of beans which is grown and harvested twice in an agricultural year. This is so despite the sophisticated technology used to plant and harvest beans. Vorster's eldest son uses an expensive modern harvester for the major part of bean harvesting. The harvester is so costly that no other individual farmer in the northern Tuli Block owns one. But despite its advanced technology, the harvester is still inadequate for doing the job fully. It leaves behind bits of crop which must be hand picked. For this reason, seasonal labour of between ten to fifteen able-bodied people, mostly women, are recruited during the four months of the two harvesting seasons (December/January; April/May).

Throughout the enterprise, there is a division of labour by sex and age according to the nature of the job. In the stores, six of the eight store assistants are women, most of them in the prime of life. Vorster's explanation for this sexual imbalance is that women are more efficient than men. Part of a store assistant's job is to clean the store. Vorster believes that this duty is best performed by women. The two male store assistants are both married. I do not know whether the women are married or not but they all have children. All twelve herders are males, of course. Most of them are aged between twenty and thirty, although there are three quite elderly men of around sixty. Except for two of the elderly men, the rest of the herders are either single or live with their unmarried 'spouses'.

Seasonal labour is sometimes hard to categorise demographically because it changes from one season to another. On Vorster's ranch, however, seasonal labour does not change very much, for reasons discussed below. But because these labourers come from nearby villages, it is difficult to know more details than that they are mostly middle-aged women. The preponderance of females over males among seasonal workers is a further reflection of Vorster's confidence in a female rather than male labour force. He believes that besides being hardworking and efficient, they are also more honest than males. On their side, females seem to seek jobs more frequently than men, perhaps because they feel more pressure to feed their children, given that most of them are single parents.

The wage level of members of the workforce is related to the pattern of recruitment. That in turn is related to their place of origin. In general, those who are in some position of authority hire their own kin or friends from their home villages. As a result, most of the labour force is from nearby villages. More importantly, and with one key exception, there are close familial ties among a considerable number of workers. In a following chapter, the full implications of what amounts to a virtual embedding in kinship relationships of the firm's internal organisation will be considered: its workforce, and, in turn, separately its management, are recruited and thus bound by kinship, primarily.

For the moment, I do want to stress that there is a continuity between this capitalist firm's policy of paternalism, its familist tendency in management and the importance of local kinship networks in its labour force. A notable and thus revealing exception is the employee who mediates between the owner-manager and the workforce, namely the African foreman. This relative stranger to both management and workers, originates from Malawi. He came to Botswana as a labour migrant many years back with his friend who is employed as a cook in Vorster's house across the border in the Transvaal. Most probably, the Malawian has been put in this intercalary role deliberately so that Vorster can use him to destabilise any united action against him by the rest of the interrelated workforce. The Malawian is thus Vorster's ear on what the workforce may be planning against the family firm.

Formal education beyond mere literacy and numeracy among the workers is not valued highly or financially rewarded in Vorster's firm. Vorster himself does not have much formal education, although he reads and writes both English and his mother tongue fairly well. The management and overall supervision of his family firm rests heavily and almost solely on Vorster and the members of his family. The fact that his sons are technocrats, that among themselves they provide all the sophisticated skills needed in the enterprise, reduces and undermines the opportunity for employees to be upwardly mobile on the basis of education or technical training. Workers' wages are therefore not commensurate with education or skills but reflect the trust or relationship between employer and employee. The close supervision of work throughout the enterprise by members of the family firm obviates the delegation of authority.

There is virtually no need for a clearly defined hierarchy among the workforce. As a result the African foreman is foreman only in name. His position is so weak that, unlike on other settler ranches, his job here has no perquisite. He is not allowed to graze his cattle on Vorster's farm. Hence, the author's strong conviction that Vorster's main use of the African foreman is to spy on any clandestine activities and unsavoury expressions of the workforce. Vorster does not pay higher wages in comparison with other settler ranchers *as a matter of rule*. His paternalist tactic is that he occasionally pays high wages to an educated child of one of his protégés (someone, for example, who is waiting for a School Certificate examination result) if the job is temporary, i.e. when the worker is certain to leave shortly.

Phase two

In presenting this phase, I intend to stress some of the increasing responsibilities of Vorster's eldest son, Verlem, within the overall business of this family firm. This also brings to the fore problems that are faced more generally – how this family firm's multiple enterprise is further connected with the rest of the Tuli Block. The link is made by different family members in the performance of their various duties. More importantly, perhaps, this second half of the case documents the expansion of the family firm beyond its previous domain into a new geographical area. This occurs here when a member takes advantage of a new state-backed economic opportunity which he pursues within his own area of specialisation. In broad theoretical terms, Verlem's case shows that even though the familist firm has developed its enterprise outside the framework of the state, it does not deny itself the opportunity to benefit from a state-backed venture if a possibility arises.

Verlem is now thirty-three years old, married, and has two daughters.

His wife, an Afrikaner, is from a neighbouring farm. With a diploma from a Transvaal technical school, Verlem has the formal training as well as practical experience to enable him to repair and service all vehicles and mechanical equipment in his father's enterprise: tractors, cars, trucks, caterpillars, bore-hole engines and other farming equipment. The fact that he can do such repairs and servicing drastically reduces the cost of vehicle maintenance for the entire family firm.

Within the application of his wide technical training, Verlem's main interest has been in arable production, initially in growing groundnuts by dryland farming. Following his completion of a Limpopo river weir for the ranch, he has begun to grow groundnuts under irrigation as well. In 1986, he increased his cultivated area to more than 4,000 ha. He cleared more land on the river side of the farm in order to make full use of the weir. Verlem and his affine on the Transvaal side of the river shared the costs of constructing the weir, and now share its use. This is one instance of how the settlers are at an advantage in the use of shared resources that span the two countries, such as river water. Such bordermanship gives them benefits which are beyond the reach of indigenous ranchers who do not have considerable state backing.

For harvesting groundnuts, Verlem uses the very expensive and sophistic-ated harvester which is beyond the means of other ranchers in his neighbour-hood set. His scale of crop production makes use of the harvester economic. It may be that one reason for buying the harvester was to reduce the number of hired workers. But, as already mentioned, seasonal labourers are employed to pick what the harvester misses. The harvester is not efficient enough for the task as a whole, though it is much faster and ultimately more economic than labourers, given Verlem's large scale of cultivation. There is also a prestige aspect to its use. Its high cost makes its ownership a proof of economic differentiation among Tuli Block settlers, many of whom opt for growing maize and sorghum, both of which are produced more cheaply with less sophisticated machinery.

By offering the family's wide-ranging machinery for hire, Verlem also extends his family's influence to other settler and indigenous farmers beyond his father's neighbourhood. For caterpillar services such as bush and boulder clearing, he charges his clients £10 per hour. He is also available on hire to do other tasks which require the use of heavy machinery. In 1986, for instance, Pule, a prominent local farmer from the national elite (see Chapter 4), contracted Verlem to build him a weir across the Limpopo river, for irrigation purposes. Verlem is well spoken of by his clients who commend him for his speed and thoroughness when doing their jobs.

The settler's policy has always been to market their crops where prices are higher, be it in South Africa or Botswana. Indigenous farmers who use state resources in arable production are required as a condition for receiving such resources, to market their crops in Botswana. As I indicate in Chapter 4, this is because the aim of the state in helping them produce especially cereals is to make the country self-sufficient in the requirements of food staples. Until recently, with a Botswana government permit, Verlem has sold his groundnuts to a marketing cooperative in Potgietesrus, his Transvaal hometown, because of the higher prices and the bonus given when the cooperative of that town has made a profit. From the autumn of 1985 he has sold his groundnuts to a local cooperative in a nearby village, close to his brother's store. This has been the more profitable alternative for two reasons. First, the South African rand collapsed relative to the Botswana pula. Second, due to the 1979–85 drought over southern Africa, the Transvaal cooperative made no profit and consequently paid no bonus. Because he does not use the state credit but his own resources, Verlem is able to take advantage of higher prices for grain in either country.

Despite the higher prices of groundnuts which attracted Verlem into arable production, Botswana's priority is the production of staples like sorghum and maize. The government recently opened up state land in north-western Botswana for the sole production of staples by farmers who are given certain subsidies as incentives. The state, through its Agricultural Marketing Board, has undertaken to buy all food grain from this project. Following his youngest brother's completion of a diploma in agriculture in the Transvaal and his subsequent return to the Tuli Block, Verlem left for north-western Botswana to take up the challenge to produce food staples.

THE CLARK FAMILY FIRM: FROM SPECULATOR TO TECHNOCRAT

The Clark family firm has a history which, perhaps more than any other in the Tuli Block, illuminates an extreme in the development of ranching among settlers of English origin. It is the extreme which culminates with expansion into the most highly specialised ranching and without any diversified portfolio in wholesaling, trading stores or secondary services. This culmination brings with it, ultimately, the liquidation of the firm itself. The contrast to Vorster's family firm is striking. Vorster's family firm, as I have shown, reaches its peak with a collective emphasis on the undivided firm under the family head. The members of that capitalist family firm see themselves to be keeping up, in their familism, an Afrikaner way of life.

The Clarks, like other settlers of English origin (cf. Benson's profile following this one) take individualism within the family firm for granted. They do not operate the family firm as a collective among adult members under a family head. Instead, at their peak, in accord with their individualist version of a capitalist ideology, they form a company, with each member being a shareholder. In their efforts to get the most profit they maximise their autonomy, even at the cost of having to liquidate the company.

Although important, the case histories of Vorster's family firm and the Clark family firm differ in much more than ethnicity. The differences documented extend to personal networks, to lifestyles, to management practice, to firm organisation, among other things. The presentation of the case of the Clarks is also somewhat different as it is important to bring the contrast between the family firms into perspective and to give needed evidence on the extreme development of ranching among British settlers. Hence, in the Clarks' case, the case is presented in phases, not so much according to generations as in the first case, but according to the level of development of the enterprise. This development is from the lower level of minimal specialisation and non-professionalism, the level of cattle trading and speculation, to the higher, specialised level of exotic breeding: the first is achieved during the colonial period, the second more recently in the post-colonial phase.

Phase one

It is useful to have an image of the ranch in mind. For this reason, I begin with a description of the social spaces of the ranch and the styles of living that go with such spaces.

The ranch, with a measurement of 15,000 ha. has two farmhouses, some three miles apart. One is the mansion built for the firm's founder, Arthur, and kept by his son, Brian. It was built in stages, rooms and sections being added on with the growth of the family and the increasing prosperity of the family firm. Such stage by stage building is usual for main houses on ranches, as I indicated in the presentation of the familist family firm. Following an architect's plan or completing a whole house at once is rare, the exceptional instances being additional houses. Brian was immensely proud of his mansion, whose building he had himself supervised over many years. When he showed me around it, from room to room, he boasted that if it was just outside Johannesburg, it would be worth 200,000 pula (£66,667).

The large scale of the family firm's business at its most successful point is reflected in the vast size of this mansion. It is bigger and somewhat more elaborate than Vorster's. Indeed, for the Tuli Block, it verges on being a stately home and is certainly the biggest and best-kept of the settler houses, apart from that of the recently-arrived Mulder. There are great reception rooms for entertaining; the screened verandah has more chairs than the foyer of a major hotel in Botswana's capital; fine marble decorates the walls and the floor and an extension of the house serves as a well-equipped office. Nearby are two large fuel containers with a capacity of a thousand gallons. There is a television and short-wave radio mast which is said to be adequate for communications with another ranch owned by the same family sixty miles away in the Transvaal. Tall gum trees and a sizeable, lush green lawn, a costly luxury in Botswana, surround the front of the mansion. What the mansion reflects above all is the public eminence achieved by the firm's founding father, Arthur, as something of a settler spokesman and notable.

The second and lesser house on the ranch is where Brian's own son, Charles, lived as the Clarks' last manager. The original owner of the lesser house built it and then sold it along with the surrounding farm, which the Clarks merged with theirs. Charles did not take over the mansion when he eventually took over the management of the ranch (for a contrast, see Bennett, 1979: 221 on the practice of house exchange at succession among ranchers in the North American Plains at the turn of this century). A ranch owner's house usually overshadows that of the manager, and so too here, despite an apparent transfer of ownership. Keeping back the mansion reflected Brian's reserving authority and a veto over major decisions, if not day-to-day running of the ranch. This was so even when he was in his early seventies and had assigned his property through a Deed of Transfer to a company belonging to his children.

Charles's house, which is much smaller and simpler than the great house, has a vegetable garden. Virtually all settler farms have a vegetable garden, sometimes known as a kitchen garden. Such gardens are very important to the settlers because they give them a fair measure of self-sufficiency in vegetables.

At one time, the great house was an important centre for sociality. Its facilities compensated for the general lack of clubs and other places of social entertainment in the Tuli Block. On the verandah, for example, was a darts board on which family members and visitors played, usually in the evenings or during week-ends. For music, there was a grand piano, which looked more impressive than any other piano I saw in the Tuli Block, such as that in Vorster's house.

The leisure spaces on the ranch were reserved for settlers and other European visitors, primarily. On this farm, unlike on that of Vorster, African visitors were also acceptable for purposes of companionship and relaxation in a number of instances, such as on the many occasions when the country's first president, who also had a large farm nearby, visited the family. African visitors and some Europeans met the settler ranchers in the work space as well as in the private recess. This was not true in the case of Vorster's farm. For the less prominent visitors to the Clark family firm, however, a house-maid, acting as a go-between, would call the settlers to come from their leisure space. This was the treatment that was given to the workers too. Only there, outside the house, would they meet and talk with, for example, the African foreman or with the agricultural demonstrator who served the adjacent communal area and sometimes came on matters affecting his own area and the freehold. Even so, this family firm was more open to visitors than was that of Vorster.

Housing for the foreman and herders was provided by the workers themselves, not on the ranch but nearby in the communal area just outside the farm's perimeter fence. The workers' mud huts were neglected, poorly thatched or roofed with bits of cardboard. The workers, Khoisan apart from the Damara foreman, lived in a squalid hamlet. Originally built to be a cattlepost in the 1940s by the workers' parents or grandparents, it had the appearance of a squatter settlement. At that time the servants and herders of a member of the aristocracy of the local main tribe, poor and inferior within the wider community, were known as 'people of the chief'. Though small, their hamlet had included more people than the Clarks needed for herders so they formed a pool of labour, repeatedly being hired and fired by different ranchers, including the Clarks.

The Clarks' family firm began shortly before the First World War, when Arthur and his son Brian came from Bournemouth, England, and started farming in the Transvaal. In Botswana, to which they moved in the early 1920s, the firm's first venture was dairying, with production of cheese for export to South Africa. This was on a Gaborone Block farm bought in the 1920s with the proceeds from selling the Transvaal farm. After a few years, the venture collapsed, and no more cheese was produced by the Clark family. The failure was the result, in part, of local hazards, severe drought along with an outbreak of foot-and-mouth disease, in part the impact of the world-wide depression of the 1930s.

Further change then came with the boom in the Johannesburg cattle market and, in turn, the boom in the export of cattle from Botwana. The Clark family firm responded, as did other settlers including Vorster's family, by expanding its lucrative speculation in cattle bought for fattening from Africans in Botswana's tribal reserves. This expansion required two further investments, in building first a bigger ranch and then trading stores, at least one within the reserves.

The basis for the first investment was made in 1938. The well developed Gaborone farm was sold, and 4,500 ha. of virtual bushland in the Tuli Block was bought from an absentee owner. The tract had first become commercial land under the ownership of the Bechuanaland Exploration Company. The last absentee owner had been an Afrikaner, one of many forced to abandon farming and return to South Africa in the wake of the depression. What the Clarks took over, from their viewpoint, was deserted wilderness, although in fact it was sparsely settled by Africans. To turn it into a major fattening ranch, more land was needed. Hence Arthur added the two adjacent ranches, another 4,900 ha., which he bought in 1945 on returning home with his pay from the war. It can be seen from this account, as from that of Vorster, that remuneration from the First and Second World Wars provided valuable cash impetus in ranch purchasing.

Works on a considerable scale had to be completed, in the event, largely under the supervision of young Brian. Nearby villagers were hired to do the construction. Having learned to speak the local language, Setswana, in the south, Brian was able to supervise them. The workers were originally immigrants from the Transvaal, Brian pointed out to me, making a show of local knowledge. Their tasks included: the construction of the perimeter fence to replace painted rocks that had been previously used as the farm boundary; the hand-digging of wells for livestock and domestic water needs; and the building of the first two rooms of the main farm house. There had been no house at all on the farm, and a tent had had to be pitched to accommodate the Clarks at first.

Some idea of Brian's personal development at this time can be gained from the fact that in 1933, the year he married a distant cousin, he completed a Junior Certificate. This gave him a formal educational qualification of a high order, relative to that of his farmer contemporaries. His wife had been a clerk in the Bechuanaland Protectorate government in Mafeking, South Africa, where she was born. It is worth noting that in his old age Brian liked to give the impression of having learned primarily not from formal education but from people and experience. This was the main point, also, of the heroic stories about Brian and his local knowledge which his university educated son told me.

For the second investment, in 1939, the Clarks bought one store in a very large village fifteen miles away, and they established a second store near the farm gate. For most of the next thirty years these stores were a source of vast profit. Through the stores the Clarks were brought into close contact with African cattle producers and gained local knowledge that was valuable for speculation. In times of major disaster, such as drought or a foot-and-mouth epidemic, the Clarks were well placed to buy hundreds of cattle cheaply through the stores. The village store was sold in 1968 when the government increased cattle prices by 12 per cent and speculators were forced to raise their purchase prices accordingly. The government's concerted effort to promote marketing co-operatives put an end to the farm-gate store in 1974: it lacked sufficient trade in grain. In periods of drought during the colonial era, settlers had exchanged cattle for grain. This had placed them at an advantage in relation to the Africans. The move by the government to widen the scope of cattle marketing resulted in the closure of many settler stores. Only the wholesalers such as Vorster were able to continue trading through stores (see Hubbard, 1983: 240, for a fuller discussion on stores in the colonial era).

Having two stores at first suited the division of labour within the family firm. Arthur himself was conscripted in 1939. But Brian's wife bought cattle from Africans at the village store in the reserves, while Brian himself did the same at the farm gate store in the commercial area. Their foreman, whom they had brought from the Gaborone Block, assisted them in turn. The arrangement was intended to enable Brian to supervise the major tasks in ranch development.

During the peak years of the cross-border trade, 1939 and 1942–9, the turn-over sustained was vast, constant and fairly rapid. It took the foreman about six days to deliver a large consignment of cattle: trekking forty-five miles from the Tuli Block ranch to the railhead in the south and then railing them for delivery to a holding ranch in Molopo, some 200 miles further on, near the southern border of the country. Within that time, he recalls, the Tuli Block ranch would normally be fully restocked, once more, with cattle bought from Africans.

The actual marketing of the cattle from the ranch, like the overall export cattle trade, was controlled from South Africa. Tuli Block farmers worked hand-in-hand with Johannesburg-based financiers who supported the cattle-buying industry. The effect of this cooperation, in which financiers acted in their own interests and contrary to government regulations, was to alter the pattern of cattle movement from Botswana to South Africa as laid down by the government in Botswana. Government regulations had directed that cattle from farms cross the frontier at a border post nearest to the farm. But at the direction of the cattle financiers, the Ramatlabama border post in southern Botswana was used by the Clarks for their marketing.

This was contrary to government regulations as their ranch is north not only of this but also of another border post. It would have been expected that the firm would use one of the border posts north of the Ramatlabama one, closest to its own farm. The apparent irregularity arose because the South African financiers, who backed Tuli Block farmers with capital, dir-ected the movement of cattle for market through the border posts which they considered least congested. Through this family firm, the financiers rented a cattle-holding ranch in Molopo, where they received cattle deliveries from the firm's African foreman. The control of the financiers from their Johannesburg base was in accord with what Hubbard calls the 'reserve nature' of Botswana's cattle industry at this time in history (Hubbard, 1983: 119). (See further discussion later.)

The involvement of the Johannesburg financiers in the cattle trade of settler farmers in Botswana came to an end under the impact of South Africa's sanctions against the Protectorate's cattle exports from 1939–41. The effect of the sanctions upon the Clarks was to make them lose support and money when the Johannesburg financiers refused to bear the burden of renting the cattle-holding ranch in Molopo. The family firm reacted to their predicament in an unexpected manner; they bought the 7,400-ha. ranch in 1944, hoping that the sanctions would soon end, whereupon, they would be able to continue their cattle trade with South Africa. When the end of sanctions came after World War II, the firm did very well and the Clarks' expansion into a second ranch beyond the Tuli Block was thus similar to Vorster's early expansion within the Tuli Block itself: the circumstances depended largely upon an external factor, the manipulation of the financiers.

The Molopo ranch had a strategic importance for increasing trade and after World War II, it continued expansion of the Clarks' firm. The relative ease with which cattle were crossed into South Africa at the Ramatlabama border post gave the Clarks an advantage over settlers who, without the backing of the Johannesburg-based financiers, had to market their cattle through the more congested border posts close to their farms. In due course, the Clarks' firm was able to forge links with buyers in Johannesburg, independently of the financiers. With enough alternative buyers from Johannesburg, the Clarks no longer needed to rely upon the firm's former financiers.

The strategic value of the Molopo ranch looked to be even greater after 1946, when it became known that there were plans to build an abattoir to serve the whole Protectorate: Lobatse was to be the site, less than fifty miles from the Molopo ranch. However, although operating from 1955, the abattoir was for some years unable to handle all the cattle offered for sale under the terms of its monopoly over the export of beef as well as livestock on the hoof. Hence, during this period the Clarks were not able to realise their hopes of taking advantage of closeness to the abattoir. The Clarks' lack of adequate family labour, which I discuss more fully in describing a later phase, exacerbated the situation and in 1969, shortly before Arthur's death, the family sold the Molopo ranch.

I have, so far, associated the development of this family firm with South African finance. The shift was from control by South African finance to greater autonomy and yet sustained dependence upon the Johannesburg market. What must now be seen is the firm's special relationship to the state, first to the colonial state and later to the post-colonial one. It was a privileged relationship, tied to public service and political influence, yielding valuable information, windfall profits and technical advantages for the firm. From one generation to the next, the Clarks had the benefit of being insiders, first because of political office and later because of professional ties with the bureaucracy of the state.

On the Protectorate's European Advisory Council, Arthur served as the elected member representing the entire Tuli Block for over a decade. In order to further protect his anonymity, dates will not be specified, but it was at a time when the influence of the Tuli Block farmers upon the Protectorate's officials was probably at its peak. A prominent, prosperous and effective spokesman for settler interests, Arthur had access to the inner circle of senior officials in the Protectorate. His reputation made him a person these officials felt they could rely upon. He was well placed to receive inside information, early, about speculative opportunities due to shifts in state policy. Having Arthur and his son Brian working together meant that the family firm had both the man of public affairs and the man of practical entrepreneurship working in co-operation.

The Clarks' firm benefited again in 1961, when drought hastened the collapse of the Commonwealth Development Corporation (CDC) project in the north-east of the country. Though on the verge of a break-even phase of development, the CDC decided to cut its losses and abandon the project. A farm in Molopo was preferred as a holding ranch for cattle. The policy shift was costly. Thousands of cattle, much household furniture, guns, numerous farm machines, such as tractors, pumps, fencing tools as well as materials, were included in this extensive CDC project. All of that vast property was sold to the Clarks by the CDC at give-away prices. According to Brian's account, he was the one who actually made the most of the opportunity, occasionally with help from his sons on their school holidays. The farm itself was rented to the Clarks for three years to allow them time to sell or remove the cattle, furniture and machines. Following the usual pattern in the north-east, the market for the cattle was in Zambia. The Clarks' African foreman trekked them to the border with Zimbabwe, where they were collected by Zambians. The farm equipment transferred to the Tuli Block was used by the Clarks for upgrading the infrastructure of their ranch.

The Clarks were in a sense the real heirs of the CDC project in north-east Botswana. What that colonial project fuelled was the development of the settlers' own ranch. By itself the windfall from the collapse of the state development project was a necessary but not sufficient condition. It was essential, but it was not to boost the family firm's Tuli Block ranch to a level of development that was higher than that of its neighbours in the same commercial area. The point is, however, that the boost did not come from capital accumulation simply due to trading and ranching within the Tuli Block. The later specialisation by the family firm in producing exotic cattle breeds owed much to a state subsidy, somewhat hidden and originally unintended as that was. It owed much also to a sudden and, in the long run, perhaps irrational decision of technocrats and planners: the abandonment of a feasible project. It could be said, therefore, that the extreme of breeding development reached in the Tuli Block was largely the outcome of the wastage of state resources elsewhere.

It is a commonplace that the death of a family firm's founder, especially one who has a dominant, pioneering personality with a considerable public reputation, brings about a crisis. It is a crisis that usually goes beyond the obvious difficulties over inheritance and the devolution of an estate. As a result, some members of the family firm put an end to their interdependence; they separate and sometimes move apart, creating not only social but physical distance between themselves. The Clarks were no exception to this. Following Arthur's death, his eldest grandson, who had had some impact on the management of the firm's expansion, took his share of the estate, left the country to farm in Zimbabwe and married and settled there. Arthur's African foreman, the mainstay of the firm's labour force, especially trustworthy in looking after the Molopo ranch, also left. The loss of both together meant a significant shortage of critical labour for the firm at a time when it was beginning to encounter serious difficulties.

Whether in the short term or the long, these were difficulties linked to changes in the wider political economy at the end of the colonial period and the early post-independence period, the mid-1960s to the early 1970s. Because of the short-term difficulties already mentioned, it seemed opportune at this time not only to sell the Molopo ranch, but to use the proceeds to give the Clarks' firm a foothold across the border. There was a risk, which the family saw, that the policies of the post-independent state might have an unfavourable impact upon settler ranching. To reduce that risk, a South African farm was bought some eighty miles from the border, and put under the management of Brian's second son, still within the family firm.

The long-term difficulties were mostly due to the impact of certain state policies on ranchers as fatteners and speculators. These policies brought about a fall in profits from cattle ranching. In 1968, a 12 per cent increase in price to the benefit of the producer in the communal areas was enforced by the state. Cattle speculators also lost out because state-sponsored marketing co-operatives took cattle trade away from them, and there was even greater risk for the speculators in the available trade, because of the Botswana Meat Commission's inability to take all the cattle offered for sale at the abattoir.

In response to these difficulties, the Clarks' firm maintained its own basic policy of pursuing advantages from the state and accommodating to state-backed projects. This time, the opportunity was state backing for a guaranteed market in pure exotic breeds. To capture a share of that market, perhaps a bigger share than that of any other Tuli Block firm, the Clarks needed substantial capital and had to liquidate some of the firm's fixed assets. The two stores, no longer so worthwhile, given the decline in fattening and speculation, were sold to raise capital for buying exotic breeds. The Tuli Block ranch was converted to full specialisation in the pure breeding of exotic cattle. No further purchases of cattle from the communal areas were brought to this ranch. Indeed, the direction of the trade, though not of the major profit, was reserved. The ranch produced some cattle, pure-bred exotic bulls, for sale to the communal areas.

In this production of exotic cattle, the firm had the further advantage of its international strategy of spreading risk. Using the South African ranch, the Clarks's firm was able to draw upon the resources of that country's more advanced agriculture. The Tuli Block ranch thus gained feed, subsidised by the South African state. It also gained a holding ground with access to the best veterinary services and from which to import brahmans and other exotic breeds into Botswana. Moreover, a member of the family actually living in Botswana could claim residence on the South African ranch. This made it possible for him to join the South African Farmers Association and be entitled to the benefits of membership of it. Such membership was particularly valuable for a specialist in exotic breeds, since it facilitated savings on the purchase of cheaper yet high-quality breeding stock.

Phase two

This response in specialisation and bordermanship marks the beginning of the firm's second phase. In discussing it, the career of Charles, Arthur's technocratic grandson is as important as were the careers of Arthur and Brian in the first phase. In my view, Charles was the most active force in remoulding the family firm and in moving its development towards the higher level of specialisation. It was partly at his instigation that the family firm was eventually turned into a company, with himself as the paid manager of its Tuli Block ranch and with other members of the family receiving shares from the profits.

Four related interests have to be brought together in order to appreciate Charles's career as a technocratic rancher. The first concerns professionalism, the advanced and technocratic training that equips a rancher to compete successfully for new opportunities in an innovative political economy. The second is the social links which are effective and expedient for successful ranching, the third arises from the cyclical nature of the climate to which all present forms of agricultural production in the Tuli Block are vulnerable and finally, our interest is in a contradiction which appears to be inherent in a certain type of capitalist family firm when it becomes a company with absentee shareholders.

The first professional training Charles received was at a South African university, where in 1970 he completed his degree in agriculture. Charles, like his father Brian before him, was thus highly educated in comparison to most of his contemporaries among the settler ranchers. The post of animal production officer in Botswana's Ministry of Agriculture was his first upon qualifying at the university and he remained in the ministry for only a year. Manager of the grazier scheme at the Botswana Meat Commission, a parastatal post even more beneficial to the family firm, then became open to him, a post he kept for some six years. Later, with the formation of the family firm as a company, he managed its Tuli Block ranch until that had to be sold in 1986. During this period, his father, Brian, remained a signatory of the firm's bank account, but drew only as much money as he needed personally and gradually handed over virtually all authority to Charles.

For the Clarks' family firm the grazier scheme was a particular opportunity, given Charles's management post in it. The grazier scheme was designed as a parastatal agency to assist cattle producers in Botswana in the wake of the 1972-3 drought. It had come to the notice of the abattoir that farmers were sending in thin and immature stock. The intent of the scheme was to provide capable farmers with immature and lean cattle from the BMC which they were to fatten and grow to maturity for sale back to it. Charles's management post enabled him, quite legitimately, to help restock the family's ranch with grazier scheme cattle. In this way, Charles, like his grandfather Arthur before him, used his public office and inside knowledge of a state sponsored development project to promote the family business.

During his term as manager of the family farm, Charles extended his social links far and wide. His South African born wife, a daughter of an English dentist whom he married while he was still studying in South Africa, often had friends and relatives visiting her from Johannesburg and elsewhere in South Africa. An active member of the South African Farming Association, Charles read South African farming journals and kept in regular contact with numerous farmers in that country. On the basis of connections with pedigree producers in the United States, he visited a Texas ranch in 1983 to study the breeding of the world-famous bison, the Santa Getrudis.

In Botswana, Charles maintained a wide circle of acquaintances with state officials, among whom he achieved a reputation for being a progressive, highly respectable rancher. Their regard for his expertise often led them to invite him to give talks in state-sponsored agricultural seminars. He had further advanced his reputation for sophistication by being the only individual Tuli Block rancher (apart from Tuli Block ranches owned by the Botswana Development Corporation, a parastatal body) to make use of a state computer kept at the headquarters of the Ministry of Agriculture by feeding data about his firm's cattle into it. Feeding the computer with the necessary information from an up-to-date ranch census, he was able to decide on the best time for weaning each calf and then for selling the mature beast. His own pride in this achievement was great; he made a point of displaying and explaining to me reams of computer print-out. His public reputation and contacts led to his being recruited to serve on the board of the Botswana Meat Commission.

Here a direct benefit for the family firm was the knowledge he gained of the loopholes in the issuing of quotas for sale cattle. His contacts and reputation for a high level of sophistication also counted further in his favour; they helped him to secure a contract from the state to supply pure-bred exotic cattle. The standard required is high and Charles inspired the officials with confidence in his ability to meet and maintain their requirements. In short, Charles's upright and progressive reputation which, like that of his grandfather Arthur, was clearly deserved, brought the family firm economic advantages.

Besides this spread of social links and public reputation, further development of the ranch depended upon technical expertise, planning of improvement in the infrastructure of the ranch, careful day-to-day supervision and, of course, substantial resources. In this development, Charles followed in the footsteps of his father, Brian, who supervised the basic work of building the ranch. Charles's part was similarly managerial, though, of course, technically more advanced. The standard of the 15,000-ha. ranch had to be raised to establish the pure exotic breeds of cattle and maintain them as a largely self-sustaining herd. The range had to be regulated better. More provision had to be made for separating stock by type, size, colour, possible disease control and so forth. To achieve that, paddocks had to be increased from nineteen to thirty-four, a very large increase and an expensive undertaking. Much of the material Charles needed, such as wire, was already available on the ranch. The paddocks and other infrastructure were built using some of the firm's windfall from the collapsed CDC project in northern Botswana.

Once the improved infrastructure was completed, the major herd of pure-bred stock was introduced, after having been kept on the Clarks' South African ranch and bought cheaply from South Africa through Charles's membership of the South African Farmers' Association. Scientific monitoring of the herd was then accomplished through the Ministry of Agriculture and Charles's circle of technician friends, with the aid of the national computer. The progress of the enterprise was evaluated over time accurately, easily and in careful detail. Comparison was made of the actual performance of the exotic breeds with certain ideal coefficients, including the expected weight of a calf at birth, at weaning and so forth. Account was taken of the lag between expected time at birth and sale and actual time. All of this was important for optimal calculations of costs, investments and profits, according to the type of breed, whether brahman, chariolais or siemmentaller.

In the Clarks' locale the communication facilities are much better suited for advanced ranching than in Vorster's part of the Tuli Block, the distribution of these and other state services across the freehold area being very uneven. A large village with a post office is near the Clarks' ranch and was used by them. Leading to this village are gravel roads which, though untarred, are nevertheless kept in better condition than those in the heavily drained northern Tuli Block. The Clarks' ranch has a telephone and a radio for house-to-house communication, across the three miles separating its two houses.

The ranch deservedly won the reputation of being the most rationalised in the Tuli Block. More than any other Tuli Block ranch, it was known for its level of sophistication and for producing exotic breeds, apparently 100 per cent pure, that were highly prized throughout the country. Other Tuli Block ranches do produce exotic breeds, but not to the same standard and usually no more than 50 per cent pure – the cost of breeding for both exotic bulls and cows being too high for most ranchers. Instead, ranchers resort to crossing a pure exotic bull with local cows and this disqualifies them from the kind of contract which Charles won for the Clarks from the state. There has been enough threat of competition, however, to constitute some pressure on Charles to keep up very high standards in order to maintain the firm's lead in pure breed production.

The rationalisation of the Clarks's ranch had less of an impact upon the size of their workforce than a subsequent drought did. The total number had dropped from more than twenty-five in 1979 to seventeen workers in 1985. Of these, two were housemaids, one for each of the two farmhouses and a third was the foreman in charge of the rest of the workforce, who were all herders. In addition, temporary workers were hired occasionally to do casual jobs, such as fence repairing, trench digging and so forth.

It was the foreman's job to clean the troughs in each paddock for feeding and watering before the cattle entered. According to his instructions, herders had to move cattle to a particular paddock on a specified date. Different types and sub-herds of cattle grazed and rotated through different paddocks. The herd was divided into sub-herds of fifty, each in the charge of a herder who was responsible for reporting any losses the same day to the foreman. Failure to report was cause for being fired. The value of the exotic cattle was so high that constant vigilance was demanded. (I heard many complaints from Charles who disparaged his present herders for their laziness and unreliability.) The foreman was also responsible for checking to find snares. Often placed on empty paddocks by herders and people from a nearby village with the aim of catching game, the snare sometimes caught and maimed cattle. Again, part of the punishment for a recognised culprit was firing and, in the case of a villager, prosecution in the village court, with the possibility of a sentence for lashing.

The workers, apart from temporary ones, were in a sense marginal, disadvantaged and without access to alternative jobs other than herding. Being Khoisan, apart from the headman, none were members of the country's ethnic majority; none had much schooling and the present foreman, an immigrant Herero from Namibia, had never been to school. Their wages were low, an average per herdsman of £7 per month, paid on a daily basis, along with a monthly ration of 12.5 kg of mealie meal for single herders and 25 kg for married ones. As is the rule on settler owned ranches, workers were forbidden to take milk from the cows. As is discussed in Chapter 4, milk is taken without restriction on locally-owned ranches. The foreman's monthly pay was £20, along with a ration of 25 kg of mealie meal. In addition, he was allowed to graze his six head of cattle on the ranch.

Having considered the importance of professionalism, of technical development and of social links, I turn now to consider some implications of a climatic cycle. The roughly twenty-year drought cycle reached its worst at a very inopportune time for the rationalisation and specialisation of the Clarks' ranch; for the drought, which began in 1979, within half a dozen years of their major expansion into specialised breeding, continued through 1985. During this period the calving rate dropped from 95 per cent to below 50 per cent in 1984. The fall in income due to reduced calving was especially unwelcome, following the recent heavy increase in capital investment.

In response to the worsening drought, Charles bought indigenous cattle. His plan was to exchange the firm's exotic breeds with local animal types which survive much longer through the drought. In 1966, a pure brahman bull exchanged with eight heifers of indigenous breeds. Although at this exchange rate the firm of the Clarks would make more profit than through their normal arrangement of producing exotic breeds, the demand for pure exotic bulls is not consistent in the communal areas. Charles grazed his indigenous cattle at a Western Sandveld borehole belonging to a trusted friend, also of British South African origin. (This friend, later a business partner and the eventual buyer of the Clarks' ranch, had three boreholes and over 1,000 head of cattle around them.) By this response the Clarks fell back upon speculation and fattening, but in the communal area, rather than on the ranch within the commercial area. The ranch itself had reached the most extreme development in specialisation among settler ranches; and yet when it came to the crisis, predictable yet unavoidable under the local climate, the enterprise of the capitalist family firm was still dependent upon the production of indigenous cattle and communal land. Once again, the positive force of the communal areas in making viable even the production of exotic breeds on the best developed of freehold farms is illuminated.

Charles generated some income from speculating and fattening in the communal area. However, it was not enough to cover the recurrent costs of the ranch. Despite his strong advice to wait at least one more year for the good rains to return (which they in fact did), Charles's brother and sister forced him to sell the ranch in 1986. The turning point came when Brian and his wife were found an old people's home in South Africa, though she actually died before moving there. While Brian was still on the ranch, he was recognised to be a unifying presence. Once Brian agreed to go, apparently for the sake of his ill wife, the two children who wanted the sale heightened their campaign.

BRIEF PROFILES

Two further cases, both of them much shorter and less detailed than the two above are now presented, that of Benson, an English entrepreneur, and Mulder, an Afrikaner entrepreneur, adding emphasis and new perspectives to the substance of the material already presented. Benson's account sheds further light on the positive force of inside information for an entrepreneur who is closely linked to the machinery of the state, while that of Mulder explicates further the operation of a social network showing, in particular, the obligations of the client and the overall ambition of a patron. Jointly, these two mini-cases emphasise more clearly than the earlier two, the decisive role of the merchant component in farm-based enterprises.

Benson – the insider entrepreneur

This brief profile of ranch-based entrepreneurship describes a family firm owned by settlers of English origin. The firm, like that of Vorster, the Afrikaner, maximises the integration of ranching and merchant trading through wholesale and retail stores. The head of the firm is a settler member of a national elite. His public position gives him access to commercially valuable information, as did that of the other English settler, Arthur. But Benson uses this information selectively. He deliberately chooses opportunities of certain benefits and of sustained profitability. What he avoids is the prestigious yet risky options, such as pure breeding. The general trend followed here is discussed very broadly by Hubbard. Hubbard emphasises that with the growth of post-colonial Botswana's economy, business favoured merchant trading, especially distribution of South African consumer goods (Hubbard, 1983: 229). It would seem that most ranchers tend to follow mainstream strategies, expanding their enterprises along the direction of the expansion of the wider national economy. The success of Benson's firm, like that of Vorster, is based on wholesaling, barter and on a rural market in which the firm protects itself against competition.

Benson, a forty-three-year-old man, who is overall manager of the firm, owns it jointly with his seventy-five-year-old father. The firm is a vast body of enterprises; a 12,000-ha. Tuli Block ranch, a major wholesale premise with its own siding for a rail, a store and a hotel in a railway town, which is also the firm's headquarters. Apart from owning another ranch at Lobatse, close to the national abattoir, the firm has a large chain of village stores. Its stores are strategically sited along the routes, hundreds of miles westward to the western sandveld. Of particular importance is that this firm, like that of the other English family, the Clarks, is also registered as a family company. At the national level, Benson is an eminent public figure. He is a Board member of Debswana, the locally incorporated De Beers mining company which mines diamonds, currently the main source of Botswana's revenue. For fifteen years he has been a Board member of the National Development Bank. Benson is thus well placed to gain inside information and thus an advantageous perspective, not merely on the financial problems of livestock producers countrywide, but also on the whole economy of Botswana in both the rural and urban sectors.

Jointly with his father, Benson inherited their firm from his grandfather, who bought out his fellow shareholders around 1956. From the beginning, the firm's main business has been to deal in cattle, purchasing them from the western sandveld in the communal areas through its stores built especially for the purpose. Before the Lobatse abattoir, the firm sold cattle to South Africa via the Tuli Block and also to Zambia and Angola via the western sandveld. Benson recalls that cattle sales to Zambia and Angola did not cease when the Lobatse abattoir was opened in 1955 but continued until after Botswana's independence in 1966.

Since its establishment in 1925, the firm has always linked merchant trading with cattle buying. Many, perhaps most, of the cattle were acquired through barter, a form of exchange which the firm has not completely abandoned. While it is not quite as paternalistic with its clients as Vorster's firm is, the fact that Benson's firm operates through stores which allow customers credit facilities, has given it an unassailable advantage over its competitors, mainly the Botswana Livestock Development Corporation (BLDC). The BLDC pays cash for cattle but has no stores to supply people's daily needs, especially food. Benson's firm buys cattle from producers in the communal areas, especially around its trading hinterland and then keeps them in its cattleposts around the stores pending their sale at the national abattoir in Lobatse. Since the drought of the 1970s, the firm has not restocked its Tuli Block ranch with trade cattle. Currently, it sends cattle from the cattleposts for marketing directly to Lobatse. In order to cope with increased herds, additional boreholes have been sunk around stores.

Thus, although Benson's enterprises outwardly resemble Vorster's, Benson's use of cattleposts makes the two firms dissimilar. Cohen stresses that similarities in outward form should not be taken to imply similarities in structure or substance (Cohen, 1985: 86). Hence, the difference between the two enterprises is discussed below in considering Benson's de-stocking measures aimed at averting drought.

The drought of the 1970s changed the firm's activity on its Tuli Block farm from speculating cum grazing to producing improved breeds. Like Vorster's, Benson's firm deliberately avoids pure breeding. A stated reason for not producing pure breeds is that Benson himself does not have enough time to do it, in other words there is a shortage of family labour. The firm's employment of an experienced European manager (see paragraph on labour below) makes this a doubtful rationalisation, however. The enormous cash turnover from merchant trading would suggest that the firm can afford the high costs of pure breeding. Benson's close connection and dealings with the state could easily secure him a contract to produce for the government. Benson also knows that it is a prestigious undertaking.

But it would seem that the most compelling reason lies in the unreliable rainfall. Lack of rainfall could force the firm, if it produced exotic breeds, to take loss-making options, for example to sustain the animals continuously on purchased cattle feed (the hardship that the Clarks' firm faced), or to risk the loss of the exotic animals through theft and disease in the unfenced and uncontrolled communal areas (the option that the Clarks' firm avoided at a high cost to itself), or, as a last resort, to sell the very expensive exotic breeds at the abattoir as ordinary beef.

This last option would incur a great loss for the firm because at the abattoir the price of a carcase is determined by its weight and its meat quality, and not by its breed. Exotic breeds greatly improve the quality of meat, of course. But that is not the point. The point is that the high value for exotic breeds is determined by high demand for live animals which are expected to reproduce. Such reasoning lies behind the pricing of exotic bulls above indigenous ones. In view of this, ranchers, like ordinary cattle producers, will normally sell their breeding stock to the abattoir only after the animals have ceased to reproduce.

Recognising the need to avoid the great risks in the production of exotic breeds, Benson's Tuli Block farm focuses on the production of improved animals. The advantage of such breeds is that they are cheaper to produce, yet higher in meat quality than the indigenous. All that is required is to mate an exotic bull with indigenous cows. Mixed breeds do very well on open Botswana rangeland. They do not need as much veterinary attention as do the pure exotic types. That has enabled Benson's firm to transfer its excess cattle from the farm to the cattleposts without incurring any losses or suffering any disadvantages. This way of averting the hazards of drought is also a response to the drought-induced fall in the carrying capacity of the range on the farm. From a total of 2,000 heads on the farm in 1979, the farm reduced to a mere 900 beasts in 1986. With such a reduction in cattle numbers, the farm was probably running at a loss.

The firm, however, is a multiple enterprise with a large wholesale trading component. Hence, the ranch can be and is maintained from the profits from merchant trading. This sustained viability underscores the importance of multiple enterprise, especially in ranching. Benson himself insists that in Botswana, no rancher can survive without one or more alternative sources of income. This lesson was driven home to him during his fifteen years as a Board member of the National Development Bank. In that position he also discovered that ranchers with the greatest loan repayment problems were those without alternative sources of income. His view is that the Clarks' firm would have fared better through the drought if it had retained its stores.

In 1972, Benson's firm recruited a European manager, in order to run their Tuli Block farm better. The manager had life-long experience on South African farms. He is assisted by an African foreman who supervises eighteen herders. In the early 1980s, after serving for fifteen years as a herder on the firm's Lobatse farm, the foreman was promoted and transferred to the Tuli Block.

Wages vary markedly among the ranch workers. The manager is paid P750 per month in cash and he also receives, as payment in kind, free food for himself and his family. Since Benson is an absentee rancher, his manager, apparently because he is a European, lives in the ranch house. The common practice is that African managers do not live in ranch houses when European ranchers are absent. Benson's manager has no cattle of his own. The foreman is paid P150 per month in cash. For his payment in kind, he receives a 25 kg bag of maize meal, like other African employees on other European owned ranches, and he is allowed to graze his sixteen head of cattle on the ranch. As noted earlier in this chapter, this perquisite greatly increases the benefits to the recipient in view of the frequent drought in Botswana. Herders receive a mere pittance, P10 each month and the normal ration of 25 kg of maize meal if they are married, or 12.5 kg if they are single. The workers, like the foreman, provide their own housing of mud huts. The foreman's hut is within sight of the farm house but, as on Vorster's ranch, herders are distributed all over the ranch. Like the Clarks, Benson complains about the unreliability and the high turnover of his herders.

In general, Benson's ranch has an appearance of careful investment, of modesty in consumption, by contrast to the conspicuous consumption that is visible on Vorster's ranch. Despite the vast amount of money that circulates in its enterprise, Benson's firm, like that of others of English origin, such as the Clarks, remains outwardly simple and unsophisticated. The wholesale warehouse is made of iron sheets which have now decayed. The firm's vehicles are old models but well maintained. Rather than buy new ones, the firm chooses to repair its vehicles. Vehicle repairing and black-smithing is the main occupation of Benson's father. Their motto is 'in business, success lies in cutting down costs'. Their simplicity in clothing and in the structure of their houses is in harmony with their motto. This simplicity is addressed contextually in the following chapter.

Mulder – the industrial entrepreneur

This profile highlights the expansion into the Tuli Block by a first generation farmer, in the mid-seventies. Although an Afrikaner from the Transvaal, Mulder is not an elite when he buys his farm. Unlike most Afrikaner Tuli Block settlers, typified by Vorster, Mulder concentrates more on manufacturing, producing malt; he undertakes this activity with the encouragement and purposeful assistance of his fellow Afrikaner, a socially powerful rancher-trader who resides in one of Botswana's main towns. The manufacturing venture turns Mulder into one of the most successful entrepreneurs in the Tuli Block. His income rivals that of Vorster, the largest resident settler in the Tuli Block. Mulder builds on this success and eventually becomes a multiple entrepreneur, before losing his malt producing enterprise as a result of being undermined by his patron for breaking the rule of the social network.

At one level, Mulder's brief case demonstrates the force of social networks, illustrating in particular the benefit of a patron-client relationship as well as its constraints. This mini-case illuminates the unstated rule that must be obeyed for the pact to work. A breach of the rule results in a very sour relationship between Mulder and his patron who brings his social influence to bear in order to wreak vengeance on him. It emphasises, too, a point raised in my closing remarks of the last case study, that social networks are constructed for business, and not for mere friendship, along ethnic lines. At another level, the case demonstrates the superiority not of multiple enterprise as such, but more visibly, of industrial enterprise and middlemanship over specialised conventional freehold farming as practised by, for instance, Charles Clark. The case study is important in that it illustrates more variation in the economic activities of the Tuli Block.

Mulder, an Afrikaner aged forty-three years, is married, with two small daughters. I do not know his family background, but he came from the Transvaal, a poor man, in 1970. For a while, he and his wife were accommodated by other settlers in the Tuli Block, until Mulder rented a store in a nearby village. He was so successful that five years later, in 1975, he had two stores of his own, around the southern Tuli Block. While doing his retail business, he bought a few head of cattle and kept them in a small cattlepost near his first store. In 1975, he rented part of a 4,000-ha. farm in the southern Tuli Block from an absentee landlord who was living in the Transvaal.

The following year, a number of things happened to Mulder. His stores began to lose money following the restrictions on the mark-up imposed by the state on retail consumer goods. The ranch owner died and his widow put the ranch up for sale. Mulder acted quickly. He sold both his stores and bought the farm. The farm cost more than the proceeds of the stores. To make up the difference, he obtained a loan from a commercial bank because, as a non-citizen, he had experienced difficulties in obtaining a National Development Bank loan.

On the farm, there was a small cement floor for producing malt; but it had been disused when he bought the farm. He decided to resuscitate the production of the malt on the advice of a much wealthier fellow Afrikaner who lent him the capital for the project on condition that the project would use sorghum grown on his own farm. In effect, as Mulder came to realise, the patron was arranging a market for his sorghum. The patron set the price of his sorghum at a slightly higher level than the ruling price of sorghum in South Africa, the country where Mulder would otherwise have bought the sorghum he needed for his malt production.

The project took off well and expanded steadily. For a start the malt was sold to individual stores, but as its production expanded, Mulder sold it exclusively to wholesalers in Botswana. By 1986, the malt factory had grown so much that it had been mechanised and electrified. It employed eighteen workers, including a resident expatriate Afrikaner mechanic. Mulder had acquired three 10-ton articulated trucks for hauling the malt to wholesalers. The firm had reached a staggering turnover of P1.7 million (£0.6 million) per annum.

The expansion of the malt factory has enabled Mulder to build the most modern single-storey house in the Tuli Block. Social importance is lent to the house and the firm since the Member of Parliament for the constituency adjacent to this farm, (also a government minister), often spends the night there when touring his constituency.

Mulder has also expanded his economic links beyond Botswana by successfully exploiting bordermanship. He has been appointed the Botswana distributor for long-life milk by a South African firm. Because he has three large trucks, he was given a contract by another South African firm in 1986, to haul goods from South Africa to another African country, north of Botswana.

While Mulder is outwardly a very approachable man, he nevertheless presents an image of success. His very high standard of living is unmistakable. He drives a very expensive luxury car, as do a number of successful (and some aspiring) entrepreneurs in Botswana. It may be reasoned that as both middleman and borderman, and because he has to host distinguished guests, Mulder has to keep up a very high standard of living. Hence, his show of success is most probably not for its own sake, but is dictated by the demands of his entrepreneurial role.

Except for the engineer and the foreman, the factory labour force comes from the surrounding villages. The foreman is from a village in southern Botswana, where he was recruited by Mulder. Most probably he was recruited from far away for the same reason as Vorster's foreman and Pule's dependent manager and, as indicated in Chapter 5—to foil any plots by the rest of the workers against the entrepreneur. The rest of the workers are predominantly teenage girls who have not been able to proceed to secondary school.

The malt factory is classified by the Financial Assistance Policy office of the Ministry of Finance and Development Planning as a food-processing firm. For that reason, it receives financial assistance from that office towards the payment of wages for its workers. As a result, the wages of the malt factory workers are much higher than those of herders, which are paid solely by Mulder (cf. Pule's profile in Chapter 4). The factory foreman earns P300 per month. I am not sure of the wages of the expatriate engineer. The rest of the factory workers, whose main job is to fill up the plastic bags with malt, earn an average of P90 each per month.

On the other hand, Mulder's senior herder is paid P40 per month, while the two other herders are paid P20 each. All the three herders receive additional payment in kind of a 12.5 kg-maize meal bag per month if they are single, or a 25 kg-maize bag if they are married. In other words, the wage level of the herders on Mulder's farm is the same as on other settler farms.

3

MEDIATION OF SETTLER
ENTREPRENEURS

Commercial ranching and arable farming have developed through mediation
that links this freehold area with the communal areas on the one hand, and
South Africa on the other. Though less advanced commercially and technolo-
gically than the Tuli Block, the communal areas have been the backbone of
Tuli Block ranching. In the colonial period, under the Protectorate, when
live cattle sales to Johannesburg were the major objective in freehold ranching,
the communal areas were the major source for the commercial areas' trade
cattle. Similarly, since the establishment of Botswana's own abattoir in 1954
and since independence, the communal areas provide a market for the
improved breeding stock produced in the Tuli Block. The alternative grazing
land for commercial ranches during recent drought years in the post-colonial
era has also been in the communal areas. The connection with South Africa
has been of paramount if changing importance. No longer the main cattle
market, South Africa has remained the supplier to the Tuli Block of pure
animal breeds, agricultural machines and equipment, as well as a source of
retail goods sold through stores owned by Tuli Block farmers. South Africa
has also continued to be a market for crops grown in the Tuli Block. This
situation clearly puts the Tuli Block farmers in the position of brokers or
middlemen between two unequal economies.

The differential response of these middlemen to changes in economic
opportunity structures and in the wider political economy from the colonial
to the post-colonial period is now examined together with the importance of
entrepreneurial organisation in the mediation of the settlers. Settler enterprises are better organised than are those of local entrepreneurs. While the
state directly influences the mediation of some settler entrepreneurs, other
settlers are able to expand their enterprises considerably, without direct
state support. Clearly crucial in settler enterprise and of paramount importance, is organisation at the family level and its ability to enable settler
entrepreneurs to take the options which determine the expansion or contrac-
tion of their firms.

The decisive factor in the specialisation of the individualist firm and the multiple enterprise of the familist firm is the availability primarily of family labour. Multiple enterprise owes to the availability of family labour its power as a more enduring business strategy than specialisation, which is only comfortably handled by one family member. The difference between familism and individualism is also important for explicating the degree of commoditisation of family labour in each of the two main capitalist firms examined. The difference in styles of agricultural practice and the variation in their development patterns also partly depend on the commoditisation of family labour. Actually, labour dynamics, or more specifically the degree of commoditisation of labour and the amount of market incorporation of the firm are at the centre of the heterogeneity in farming systems worldwide. It is for this reason that in this chapter, labour is examined more closely than other aspects of mediation, especially family labour.

The different processes that some Tuli Block entrepreneurs devise in a bid to extract economic surplus are based invariably on complex combinations and interrelationships between many factors. Such factors include familist or individualist management of the firm at the family level, paternalism between the firm and its clients, the role of the state, and bordermanship.

Familism and individualism as organisational concepts were discussed in the profiles when the far-reaching force of the organisation of the firm at the family level was initially raised. In this chapter, brief reference will be made to these concepts during the analysis of other factors, namely, bordermanship discussed first; second, the role played by the state; and third, labour.

BORDERMANSHIP

Bordermanship is a concept instrumental in economically differentiating the Afrikaner from the English in their roles as ranchers in the Tuli Block. It must be emphasised that economic differentiation between the Afrikaner and the English is limited to settlers whose sole occupation is ranching. The profiles of Benson, the English rancher-trader and Mulder, the Afrikaner rancher-industrialist show that among settlers whose enterprises extend beyond ranching, the Afrikaner cannot be rated higher than the English, but to understand why the Afrikaner has an edge over the English in enterprises that are based solely or mainly on cattle ranching, it is necessary to consider bordermanship.

It is a concept that is operationalised in the exercise of strategic action, has certain features of the principles of international trade but differs from those principles in that it is operationalised by an entrepreneur who has continuous and simultaneous 'presence' in two countries. In the Tuli Block where settler enterprises are based to some extent on social networks, such 'presence' often takes the form of network members, who may be members of the nuclear or the wider family, resident permanently across the border.

As a border region, the Tuli Block relies on South Africa for its services. Even though settlers may acquire Botswanan citizenship requiring the renunciation of one's previous citizenship, they continue to be treated for all practical purposes, such as owning business and other property, as citizens of their country of origin, South Africa. Hence, in areas such as the northern Tuli Block where there are no communication facilities, settlers resort to the use of such facilities as the telephone and the post office on the Transvaal side of the border. By virtue of their placement in the Tuli Block, a borderland between South Africa and Botswana, settlers know the general trend of prices of goods and crops in both countries. To some extent their cross-border mediation inevitably results in their taking advantage of lower costs and better prices. An astute entrepreneur decides which commodity to buy from which country and which one to sell to which country.

Clearly the Transvaal is the home of Afrikaners more so than the English, who may come from a greater distance. In particular, the profile of the paternalist entrepreneur has shown that his mediation spans the two countries and brings into its network his relatives who live across the border adjacent to his farm. The construction of the weir across the Limpopo opposite Vorster's farm, done with the help of his nephew, is a case in point. Vorster's purchase of the small 400-ha. farm in the 1980s on the Transvaal side of the border directly opposite his Tuli Block farm underscores his need to forge even stronger physical links with the Transvaal. As his profile has reflected, there is at least one occasion when he has been tried in court and convicted on a charge of smuggling hides and skins from his Tuli Block farm across the border. It can be expected that settlers like him who are well placed in terms of bordermanship will be greatly tempted to engage in smuggling. Local Tuli Block entrepreneurs suspect that by acquiring the small farm across the river, Vorster was placing himself in an even better situation to carry out illicit acts of smuggling.

On the contrary, English settlers seem to have fewer family relationships of an active kind. Such relatives, where they exist, as in the case of Charles's brother, may be located too far from the border to be much use in physically building up the farm. As a consequence, Afrikaner farmers have benefited more from bordermanship than have English; and local farmers, without family connections in the Transvaal, do not appear to benefit from bordermanship in any way.

Related to bordermanship, if somewhat remotely, is the contrast in lifestyles of the Afrikaner and the English entrepreneurs. The rounded lives of the Afrikaners contrast sharply with the more spartan lives of the English entrepreneurs.

Much care has to be taken in the interpretation of appearances, especially where the aim is to read into the lifestyle, the amount of wealth or status. Renfrew criticises archaeology for falling into what he calls 'the reflectionist mode of thought' by assuming that the prestigious goods they found in some graves in Varna necessarily reflected the high status of people buried in them (Renfrew in Appadurai, 1986: 144). Arguing that such aspects of material culture may in fact be responsible for bringing about the high status, he highlights an important analytical point that high status can be achieved by the manipulation of material goods and by display of wealth. In spite of this illuminating revelation, Renfrew seems to fall short of actually providing an analytical frame for interpreting the reasons behind ostentatious display and its opposite, the hiding of wealth or status as we see it among the settlers and the local entrepreneurs in the Tuli Block.

While an explanation that is based solely on differences in ethnicity would certainly be inadequate or even incorrect, it is also clear that the difference cannot be explained solely in economic terms since the incomes of some English entrepreneurs are quite comparable with those of some Afrikaners. For example, the income of Mulder, the Afrikaner, is comparable to that of Benson, the Englishman. But the reason why Mulder and Vorster display their wealth while Benson and Charles lead lifestyles that may be described as mean has to do with the mediation. As Afrikaners from the Transvaal, Mulder and Vorster interact a great deal with entrepreneurs and their kin in South Africa. For successful dealings with their business contacts across the border, a show of success which is embodied in a lifestyle in chorus with their material means is necessary; hence, their visible opulence. Without such visible opulence, in Transvaal eyes, they risk appearing to be the poor cousins peripheralised like the 'natives' among whom they live. Settlers of English origin, on the other hand, live more private lives because they have neither similar circles of relatives nor business contacts. Of course, they too have their own family members who went to the Transvaal specifically to expand the family's enterprise. But there is no point in some of the family members trying to impress others when they jointly own the resources.

In a limited sense, the reasons for the visible opulence of the Afrikaner entrepreneurs can be compared with those that make the district elite, among local entrepreneurs, play up their wealth. Similarly, an analogy can be drawn between the spartan lifestyles of the English entrepreneurs, which is not meant to denote poverty, and the 'simplicity' of the national elites, which is forced upon them in the course of their conformity to the norms of the official positions they occupy, as is shown in Chapter 5. Of course, one cannot deny that lifestyle is to some extent idiosyncratic. But, looking beyond idiosyncracy to the determinants of basic behaviour, the main point for theorisation is that for entrepreneurs in general, social behaviour is appreciated better when viewed in the light of the needs of the enterprise.

THE STATE AND SETTLER MEDIATION

From colonial to post-colonial times, the state has played a central role in the enterprise of ranching, even though such a role can be seen more clearly in some enterprises than in others. The central role of the state in individual private enterprise is not limited to Tuli Block cattle ranching or even to Botswana. It is a common feature of development in almost every country. Equally, the impact of the state in entrepreneurial development and in giving shape to such development is increasingly being acknowledged by a growing number of scholars. According to Long, the strategies developed by the different actors and how successful they are, are influenced by resources from the state. It is for this reason, states Long, that actor-oriented studies must concentrate upon analysing the struggles that occur between these different economic and political actors (Long, 1988: 133). Writing about post-colonial Africa, Kennedy strikes the same note in his observation that since independence, the state has been viewed by various contenders for power and wealth as by far the most important source of personal and group improvement. More pointedly, and somewhat in contrast with the situation in western countries, he states that the state rather than the market, has been the area in which struggles for the control of resources has been fought out (Kennedy, 1988: 75).

The above description would seem to fit squarely the cases of two settler entrepreneurs. First is Mulder, the industrialist entrepreneur whose enterprise largely and conspicuously owes its existence, viability and expansion to the state. Second is the case of the alternative individualist firm, a clear example of a state-backed enterprise although different from that of the industrialist entrepreneur in that its dependence on state support has grown as the firm has switched from cross-border cattle trade to specialist breeding. In other words, the extent, nature and history of its dependence on the state are different from those of the industrialist firm. Yet, in spite of differences the two firms are directly dependent on the state for their enterprises. On the other hand, the multiple enterprises of Benson and Vorster do not seem to be linked directly to the state, even though they are covertly dependent on it to the extent that their success is linked to the growth of the national economy.

The ability of a group to develop a viable and stable enterprise on the strength of good organisation and social resources outside the state is provided by Long in his study of Jehovah's Witnesses in Zambia between the 1960s and the 1970s (Long, 1984: 4–5). Long documents a situation whereby the Witnesses were excluded from agricultural credit and extension facilities, and also prevented from marketing through government marketing boards, only to eventually become better off than those who had continued to lean on the state. Writes Long:

> Years later, when Zambia felt the full brunt of the deepening economic recession, which coincided with a series of breakdowns in the functioning of government services, it was the Witnesses, who had been placed outside the state system, who survived best. By this time, they

had built their own efficiently organised informal trading and credit system for the marketing of foodstuffs in urban areas and in some cases even stretching across the international border into Zaire. (Long, 1984: 5)

A conclusion to be inferred from the above case is that possibilities of a viable entrepreneurship are not necessarily tied to the state. Addressing the situation of the Witnesses, Long observes, in fact, that heavy dependence on the state may have a negative effect on a group's long-term development profile (Long, 1984 *op. cit.*). This statement may not be strong enough to explain the collapse of the individualist firm but it is nevertheless framed within the context of the firm's collapse.

The similarity between the case of Vorster, the paternalist entrepreneur, and that of Jehovah's Witnesses is striking. Both, without the support of the state, are able to develop viable and stable enterprises through efficient organisation and on the back of social resources. Not only do their enterprises survive hardships; they also expand. The extension of their enterprises across the national frontier is a sign of their growth and expansion.

In view of the above, the role played by the state in the Tuli Block livestock enterprise needs to be carefully considered. While it is clear that the state does not play a central role in each and every enterprise in the Tuli Block, it is equally clear that even among the state-backed enterprises within this freehold area, the level of state involvement is variable. In other words, the question, in the Tuli Block enterprise, is not whether or not a firm has state support. The issue, rather, is how much state support a firm enjoys. Even so, it is important to specify the sectors that receive such support. The situation of the local entrepreneurs, among whom unequal dependence on state resources is even sharper (see Chapter 4) confirms the importance of this consideration.

So far no attempt has been made to define either the structure or the operations of the state; the analysis of the local entrepreneurs where a manifestation of the variation of the state structure justifies a fuller discussion of its operations. In the analysis of settler enterprise only those aspects of the state mechanism which directly impinge upon settler enterprise and mediation are dealt with and there the focus is on the alternative settler firms.

The next step in this argument requires that reconsideration of the variation in organisation and personal relations between the alternative settler entrepreneurs, partly as foundation for a discussion of labour. First in discussing the overall adjustments settlers resident on the Tuli Block farms made in order to cope with changed economic and political structures, it can be seen that where the paternalist entrepreneur chooses one option, the technocrat entrepreneur chooses the opposite. Instead of multiple enterprise, paternalism, highly active patron-client relations and one form of bordermanship, the technocrat entrepreneur opts for specialisation in breeding, a withdrawal from patron-client relations and another form of bordermanship. The motivation for the option of specialisation in breeding comes primarily from professional training, in part prompted by the firm in a bid to assure itself a consolidated and secure place within the cattle industry.

The technocrat's case differs in management and ownership from that of the paternalist entrepreneur. Whereas the latter owns his firm and is co-manager with his sons, the farmer manages a family farm in which he is only one of the shareholders. Furthermore, it is evident that there is economic strain on the specialised firm. This strain results from the lack of alternative sources of income during the long-lasting drought cycle. For such a family farm, it is expected that the main advantage of producing pure breeds in a highly capitalised ranch will be in the stability of planned operation. While the bull subsidy scheme continues, the state assures the market. The guarantee is provided by the Ministry of Agriculture for bulls sold at the age of six months. The time of producing them is therefore very short and the threat of range degradation from increased animals is greatly reduced. It is cheap to produce these bullocks once the infrastructure is established. Hence, the venture can be both viable and profitable, even with the lower prices that the ministry pays suppliers under the bull subsidy scheme, compared to prices farmers are paid in direct sales with individual bull buyers.

The technocrat entrepreneur is connected to the state in yet another important way, also linking the firm with communal areas. He supplies cattle producers both in the commercial and communal areas with heifers under the National Development Bank re-stocking scheme. In this case he, as the supplier of heifers, sets the price. The market for heifers, unlike that of bulls, is not guaranteed. However, in rainy years, the demand for pure breeds in Botswana is so great that the National Development Bank has decided to support cattle purchasing loans for new farmers only, i.e. not for farmers who want to expand their herds (Thothe, 1985). This trend has also been to the technocrat's advantage because new farmers need more heifers than bulls. It thus suits the enterprise of the technocrat settler farmer to take part in both schemes.

Thus the technocrat's strategy, in response to the state initiative, actually reverses the past relationship with the communal areas, in at least one respect. Instead of extraction of young stock from the communal areas for fattening, the technocrat's firm produces the young stock in the commercial area for further reproduction in the communal area. The entry of the state into the relationship provides an alternative source from which the commercial producer can extract value.

To stress the importance of a capitalist firm managing its relationship with the communal areas in terms of a state-backed strategy and to emphasise what is actually the underlying continuity in response to the change in political economy is the next concern. Initially, under the political economy of the colonial state, the individualist family firm opts for speculation, focusing on fattening with the help of stores. Under the political economy of the post-colonial state, the same firm, now under technocratic management opts for the professional producers' enterprise of breeding. But through the change in mode of enterprise, the strategy has this much continuity – that it is still the state-protected and state-backed strategy which is preferred. The firm follows the state lead whether in the white-restricted cattle trade of colonial times or the present state-subsidised breeding. Of course, there is also a shift in emphasis in terms of being mere border middlemen or border settlers. In general, the individualist firm seems to shift away from the middleman emphasis and towards the settler in that the firm is not so much a link to the market. The firm mediates on behalf of the communal areas for production and not for marketing. This role is because of South African contacts and information resources, as well as technical expertise.

In order to create a context for the ensuing analysis, it is necessary to distinguish between a settler-oriented enterprise and one that is middleman-ship-oriented. This requires a glance back into the history of settler mediation. Before 1930, when settlers came into the Tuli Block, they were not allowed to buy scrab cattle from the communal areas. Until after the recession, in 1933, they were required to produce cattle on their farms. At this time, they were, in their role as cattle producers, not middlemen but truly settlers. But when they switched from cattle production to cattle trading after the recession, they assumed the role of middlemen because they were now operating between the producers in the communal areas and the consumers in the South African mines and hospitals. According to Bonacich, middlemen who are found between producers and consumers are absent from industrial entrepreneurship and investment in the kind of agriculture that ties up capital (Bonacich, 1973: 583–5).

There is some distinction between Tuli Block middlemanship and middle-manship as contextualised by Bonacich. In the situation that he contextualises, which is typical of middlemanship in general, the broker does not have to invest heavily in overheads as would a producer. But the case of the Tuli Block farmers is that they began as producers, and proceeded to the stage of brokerage or middlemanship in response to the market. In their role as producers they had already invested in their farms, which were clearly 'the kind of agriculture that ties up capital', to borrow Bonacich's words. The kind of middlemanship that they entered into as cattle traders was very much based on their farms. The ranch thus became expedient in cattle brokerage. It is important to keep this point in mind because it is as central to the understanding of the various issues connected with settler mediation as it is in distinguishing between settler and local mediation. As is shown in subsequent chapters, an important feature of local mediation, especially among the elite, is that it is not based on the farm.

As stated above, the individualist firm shifts away from middleman emphasis and more towards settler. On the contrary, the familist firm retains the middleman emphasis with implications on the condition of the farm. In order to produce the highly valued but environmentally-sensitive exotic breeds, the individualist firm invests heavily in the development of the farm. Such development takes the form of increased paddocks, an exercise which in turn requires a more elaborate water reticulation system. This is a costly exercise by any scale. Animal production scientists argue that paddocking is not an effective way of raising management levels of animal production; hence, in Australia and other better-developed sub-tropical rangeland areas of the world it has not been implemented to the same extent as it has been in southern Africa (Grossman, 1988: 27).

It is possible, therefore, that the individualist entrepreneur has over-invested on his farm, such that the returns from the developments he has made may not give him as much profit as he might get if he optimises the level of farm development. By contrast, the familist entrepreneur, who mantains his middleman emphasis, avoids specialist breeding and consequently does not invest as much in the development of his farm. It would appear, therefore, that in his bid to pitch a high standard of livestock production aimed mainly at retaining his envied state-backed niche in the livestock industry, the technocrat entrepreneur over-invests in farm development, to his detriment. The profile of Kgari, the aristocrat entrepreneur also lends support to the view that over-investment in the condition of the farm may lead to economic loss.

Taken in its wider context, the contrast in the level of investment between middleman and settler enterprises is a reflection of the superiority of multiple enterprise over specialisation in entrepreneurial terms. Multiple enterprise avoids over-investment in any single venture. On the other hand, even the optimal amount of investment required for specialisation in a single enterprise would still exceed that deemed necessary for the same venture if it were part of a multiple enterprise.

Some comparison may be made between middleman/settler roles on the one hand, and craftsman/entrepreneur on the other. Generally, a settler role can be compared with craftsmanship because it took certain skills to do farming the way it was done especially in the early days in question. A middleman role is comparable to entrepreneurship because both are brokerage roles. Thus an entrepreneur differs from a craftsman in that the latter has to be some kind of artisan while the former is understood to be someone who takes risks in order to take advantage of whatever opportunity might arise in business.

In the economic roles of the Tuli Block settler farmers, this distinction is not always manifested as distinctly as defined here. In their case, it is only a question of emphasis of one role or the other and even then, the emphasis changes from time to time as the settlers adapt to altered economic situations. Adaptation to new conditions suggests they are entrepreneurs, but their history in the Tuli Block and before they came into this commercial area portrays them also as craftsmen. In other words, they seem to be simultaneously craftsmen and entrepreneurs. Local farmers, because they are newly arrived in the Tuli Block and because of their unmistakable lack of ranching skills (as shown in Chapter 4), are clearly entrepreneurs and by no means craftsmen. Some of them make up for their lack of ranching skills by hiring highly-skilled European labour on local farms. For local farmers, such use of commoditised labour has the effect of undermining their need to be craftsmen while simultaneously increasing their role as entrepreneurs (see also van der Ploeg, 1990: 272).

CONTRAST IN THE PROCESSES OF EXTRACTING ECONOMIC SURPLUS BETWEEN THE ALTERNATIVE SETTLER FIRMS

The last section addressed the role of the state in the enterprise of the individualist family firm. This section analyses the processes through which entrepreneurs as settlers and middlemen profit by mediating between the co-existing capitalist and non-capitalist modes of production. Such analysis, contrasting the alternative settler firms, aims to illuminate the evolution of different processes of extracting economic surplus between the two firms, predicated by the different circumstances of their mediation. Any useful study of mediation in Botswana must recognise the interdependence that cross-cuts the modes of production, however much they appear to be separated in different areas, commercial and communal. It has already been suggested that a transformation is in progress. At the turn of this century, the commercial area, Tuli Block, depended for its survival on the communal area of the reserves, whereas currently, the relations of dependence have become more mutual, though still unequal. In this section it is shown how entrepreneurs continue to dominate the relations of the communal areas with the Tuli Block through unequal exchange.

Having established the social relations appropriate for a clientele in the communal areas, a paternalist entrepreneur uses barter as an economic method of unequal exchange and therefore of extraction of economic surplus. The use of barter is a carefully thought-out strategy, with many advantages for the entrepreneur, as can be perceived from the quotation below. Appadurai defines barter as:

> the exchange of objects for one another *without* reference to money and with maximum feasible reduction of social, cultural, political or personal transaction costs. It may be regarded as a special form of commodity exchange, linking exchange of commodities in widely different social, technological and institutional circumstances. (Appadurai, 1986: 9)

Whereas some may view barter as an old-fashioned form of transaction which cannot be expected to operate in a modern economy, it is actually on the increase in the contemporary world. Appadurai states that in the United States alone, the value of bartered goods in 1986 was US$12 billion (Appadurai, 1986: 10). An essential characteristic of barter is that it is a response to trade barriers. In chapter one, mention was made that the Tuli Block and its surrounding areas occupied by the clientele of the settlers are isolated from the rest of the country. Such isolation creates a barrier for the local community in its efforts to trade with centres away from its own locale, and places the paternalist entrepreneur in a most advantageous position to do bartering with it.

The value of the cattle exchanged with such goods as ploughs and donkey carts is more than the value of these goods. Yet the cattle producers perceive that it is more convenient, quicker and, in social terms, safer to exchange their animals for goods than to send them some 200 miles away to the abattoir at considerable cost and at the risk of condemnation of their meat. When in need of a tractor to plough their fields, a paternalist entrepreneur is always ready to hire them one. If a job falls vacant on his ranch or in any of his stores, he gives priority to his protégés and their nominees. When cash is needed urgently for an emergency, a paternalist entrepreneur may not lend money, but he will buy their cattle for cash, thus inducing them to sell to his advantage. If they run short of food, and have established trust and credibility, he will sell them grain from his shop on credit.

A paternalist entrepreneur even operates exchange beyond the usual trade. Thus he accepts goats as payment because the poor majority have goats. In this way, he is able to reach out to a wider clientele than he otherwise would if he only bartered merchandise with cattle.

Discussing similar relations, Meillassoux argues that the peasant sector, with its low constant capital, serves as an organic component of capitalist production; the peasant sector supplies capitalist production with the resources necessary to its survival (Meillassoux, 1978: 103). A paternalist entrepreneur clearly survives on the product of his communal clientele. His whole enterprise is based on the poor. It is the potential wealth of the poor which he saps through a relationship which, though parasitic, is projected in the symbiotic image of a haven against natural disaster. Even though on the surface the paternalist entrepreneur does not devise the exchange terms unilaterally, he is nevertheless in a much stronger position than his clients – in effect setting the unequal price unilaterally.

Meillassoux argues that prices of peasant produce are determined by the capitalist sector in a way that does not destroy the non-capitalist mode but reconstitutes it to the advantage of the capitalist mode (Meillassoux *op. cit.*). The issue of reconstitution is discussed in the section on the manner in which the paternalist entrepreneur organises his clients for his labour requirements. The paternalist entrepreneur keeps his clientele poor by expropriating through a pricing mechanism the surplus that would give them a breakthrough from a poverty trap to economic independence.

In discussion of barter as the form of economic exchange that the paternalist entrepreneur chooses, it was shown that the poverty trap of the clientele of the paternalist entrepreneur is predicated in part by the closure of their geographical locale to other commercial areas of the country. Such a situation makes them fall prey to the entrepreneurial ploy of their patron, leading to what de Janvry calls 'functional dualism', whereby the peasant sector is functionally tied to the needs of the capitalist sector through the provision of both cheap labour and cheap food (Long, 1989: 110). In the Tuli Block context such functional dualism enables the periphery to export cheap raw materials such as its cattle, goats and its labour, and the capitalist firm of the paternalist entrepreneur to maintain high rates of profit.

The clientele are quite aware of their captive condition and they are not passive to it. They try as much as they can to reduce it by establishing links with the distant commercial areas through their children who have had sufficient formal education to obtain jobs or to establish petty trade. It must be stressed, however, that their aim is not to cut the links with the paternalist entrepreneur completely; they realise the advantage of their relationship with him in spite of its inequality. What they do under the circumstances is to spread their risks by establishing social relationships with other economic set-ups as well. The idiom of cooperation between them and their patron is that they may not forge similar links with another settler within the Tuli Block, and this they avoid since they are well aware that their patron is in competition with other settlers. Nevertheless, the situation between them and their patron shows how interface conveys the idea of face-to-face encounter between individuals representing different interests, resources and levels of power. It also shows how the perceptions of the clientele and their relationship with the patron is reshaped as a result of the interaction (see also Long and Arce, 1987: 7).

The situation of a technocrat entrepreneur is quite different. His extraction of economic surplus is best understood in relationship to the state. Pure breeding is, at the moment, a state-backed production. A technocrat entrepreneur has to establish himself first as a capable breeder before he can be given a contract to produce for the state. Nevertheless, the viability and profitability of his enterprise depend on the state, which unilaterally decides what price to offer him for his animals. I have already suggested a key consideration here. The prices paid to the technocratic entrepreneur for the bulls are not competitive with what he might get from a direct sale among communal area cattle producers. But the guaranteed purchase of the state of all bulls that he produces, nevertheless makes breeding a viable and profitable enterprise.

It is important at this stage to contrast the different ways in which the alternative entrepreneurs extract or expropriate economic surplus from their mediation. The paternalist entrepreneur does this by reaping the difference in the price that he pays his clients for their cattle and goats and the much higher price that he obtains when he sells the same animals to the abattoir. He pays an average of P400 for a heifer or young ox which he in turn sells for P600 immediately thereafter, or for an average of P800 after six months when he will have grown it to maturity on his ranch. Another important aspect of mediation through which the paternalist entrepreneur extracts economic surplus from the communal areas is his use of labour networks. Since this is central to his entire mediation, it is dealt with separately and in some detail later.

The technocratic entrepreneur expropriates his profit in a different way, buying breeding stock of exotic breeds which are highly prized in the cattle industry, the most popular of which is the brahman. Because the state is promoting the sale of brahmans to local farmers in the communal areas, it gives the technocratic entrepreneur a contract to produce these exotic animals and the technocratic entrepreneur makes his profit or economic surplus by producing these exotic breeds, all of which are bought by the state.

The paternalist entrepreneur deals mainly with his clients in the communal areas, whereas the technocratic entrepreneur deals mainly with the state as his trading partner, although he deals with the communal areas through the sale of his heifers. In a bid to be successful, the paternalist entrepreneur puts up the image of a patron – a seemingly protective attitude towards his clients, while the technocratic entrepreneur has to keep his profile and esteem very high in the eyes of the Ministry of Agriculture by upholding a high standard of animal husbandry. To be prepared for possible competition with potential suppliers of exotic breeds he has to set very high standards of animal production. Because he seldom deals with cattle producers in the communal areas, his attitude towards them is not as liberal as that of the paternalist entrepreneur who deals directly with them.

The production of pure breeds in the Tuli Block has reversed the role of this commercial area in relation to the communal areas where the pure breeds are sold. As a consequence of ranch-based breeding, cattle are now also moving from the Tuli Block to the communal areas. The word *also* must be stressed because cattle still move predominantly from the communal to the commercial areas. However, for a technocrat entrepreneur, the crucial point is that he produces mainly for the state on behalf of the communal areas, but not always directly for the communal areas. Producing for the state makes the technocrat entrepreneur a protected producer who extracts his economic surplus from the state through its protection of his enterprise.

To appreciate better the effect or impact of state protection on the technocrat's enterprise, one needs to draw an analogy between the technocrat's enterprise on the one hand and the settler cattle trade during the earlier colonial period (1933–55) on the other. The settler cattle trade became viable and profitable partly because of its protection from African competition. Such protection, unlike bartering, as practised by the paternalist entrepreneur, cannot be expressed in financial terms; it can only be appreciated for what it is worth in the preservation of an economic position or niche.

The state-protected position of the technocrat entrepreneur requires consolidation on his part. As in the situation of the paternalist entrepreneur, the consolidation of the position of the technocrat entrepreneur revolves around his image in the eyes of his trading partners. Since the technocrat entrepreneur trades with the state, he has to keep his image from waning in the opinion of government officials.

This section has shown how different types of entrepreneurs as mediators have adapted to changes in the structure of economic opportunity. The distinct strategies devised by the mediators have been discussed within the contexts of their circumstances. It has also shown, without discussing either ranch viability or the viability of the whole enterprise, how farmers in their roles as middlemen create economic surplus. Different kinds of entrepreneur, the paternalist and the technocrat, use a positive image to win the confidence and trust of their trading partners. Both also depend on protection from competition for the success of their mediation.

But while the paternalist entrepreneur creates his protection from competition by creating a dependent clientele through a hierarchy of middlemen, the technocrat entrepreneur is protected directly by the state for whom he mainly produces. For both types of entrepreneur, extraction of economic surplus is linked to and associated with their protection, although the mechanism for extraction and protection is different for each type of entrepreneur. The paternalist entrepreneur extracts his economic surplus through barter from his protected clientele, and by organising the clientele to provide his labour, while the technical entrepreneur extracts his economic surplus through a guaranteed state market, which thus serves as a protection of his enterprise.

An important point is that while it does not directly link him with the communal areas, the mediation of the technocrat entrepreneur reverses the direction of the flow of cattle, which, in earlier times, was only from the communal to the commercial areas.

DYNAMICS OF LABOUR IN SETTLER FIRMS

The central importance of labour in any agricultural undertaking cannot be overemphasised. Van der Ploeg writes,

> whatever indicator is used, there is in every agricultural system considerable variation. The variation is to a considerable degree the outcome of the different ways in which the labour process is structured. (van der Ploeg, 1986: 34)

On the other hand, the structure of the labour process, which may also be termed the rural labour relations, plays a key role in the structure of rural power and prosperity (Croston, 1989: 4). In other words, labour relations are central to variation in agricultural enterprise which in turn forms the basis for social differentiation. The case material in this study shows that labour dynamics cannot be understood outside the context of social relationships upon which production in the capitalist firms of both the settlers and the locals is based.

All profiles indicate, some more clearly than others, that production in the firm is based on the labour resources of the wider community and its social structures and not only on the sweat of the hired employees. In particular, the familist firm shows that the appropriation of the surplus value of workers by the firm is framed as a social relationship between the firm on the one hand and the community on the other. The community side includes kinship networks through which unpaid or underpaid labour is supplied to the capitalist firm. Through the social relationship, the capitalist firm avoids the exchange value of community labour, extracting instead the community's use value. In the process, the labour value of the community is very much veiled and the community is not able to readily associate the product of the capitalist firm with its own labour input. For this reason, when debating the thesis and antithesis of the commoditisation model, Long emphasises that goods in a market must be analysed not only in terms of their exchange ratios, but also in terms of the amount of labour embodied in their production (Long, 1984: 9).

In this chapter as in Chapter 5, the focus is more on the processes through which different kinds of labour – family and hired – is procured and retained by the alternative entrepreneurs, and less on employee statistics. The discussion contrasts the circumstances of the two alternative settler entrepreneurs where family labour is deployed in quite dissimilar ways. In the course of the analysis which accounts for the difference, the superiority of patronage or paternalism over the technocratic mode in which there is no established social connection between the capitalist firm and its employees, is highlighted. Prestation, a mechanism for early involvement of family sons in the settler firms as a means of attracting and retaining them in the enterprise is given some coverage. Family labour is discussed first, followed by hired non-family labour.

Settler family labour

The participation of family members in family firms has been analysed by, among others, Benedict (1968), Long (1972) and Bennett (1979). A basic issue that these scholars ponder is why mature grown-up sons participate full-time in the enterprises of their parents in certain instances, while they stay away from family firms in others. One suggestion as to the reason for their participation is that the work in the family is commensurate with their own economic interests (Long, 1972: 17).

A conspicuous strategy of the familist firm is the sharing of work among family members. This contrasts sharply with the set-up in the individualist firm. Looking at the tasks done by the sons in the familist firm at its peak, one might agree that by working for the firm they fulfil their own economic interests. Because of the large scale and success of the family firm there are enough tasks and challenges for the sons.

However, such an answer is inadequate, because performing the available tasks and responding to challenges may not necessarily be a fulfilment of the economic interests of the workers concerned. This is especially so in view of the payment structure of sons in the familist firm where they do not take a salary. It is difficult to see how the system of remuneration could be said to be a fulfilment of their economic interests. Here, Benedict's observations (1968), are helpful for further illumination of the problem. Benedict examines the different ways of involving sons, the methods of obliging them to remain in the firm as well as the advantage of early child involvement in the family enterprise. He considers that keeping family members within the family firm, involves incorporating them into the family firm during their early years before they are exposed to different career possibilities and while the business is still controlled by their father who as head of the family is also head of the business. The father uses his fatherly authority (which is not challengeable by his sons at this stage) to involve his sons in the business. His main aim, however, is to make prestations. The father's prestations which demonstrate his confidence in his children, put them under certain kinds of obligations. Such early commitment to the family firm through participation as co-owners with their father and through being given not a general education but one that is specifically channelled to the needs of the family firm would seem to have been designed to bind them to the family firm. After their formal training and experience as co-owners of the stores they would not wish to work elsewhere.

However, the process is more complex than the position that Benedict presents. Instead of the sanction which he posits, on first principles, and merely on the assumed logic of the prestation, what actually operates is reward and promise of reward. The size and success of the multiple enterprise of the familist entrepreneur presents an attractive bait for his sons. The sons are conscious of the pre-eminence of their family firm among other firms in their neighbourhood. Such awareness gives them a strong sense of security, pride and an enduring interest in their family firm. And while the success of the family firm continues and the atmosphere of cooperation within the family remains unchanged, pursuing a job opportunity outside the family firm is hardly imaginable for the sons.

Yet even that is not sufficient to explain the continued interest of the sons. Underlying the whole concept of prestation and hence the success of family firm heads in retaining family labour is the crucial issue of inheritance. In the familist firm of the Afrikaner, sons hope to subdivide the family farm in accordance with the already laid down blue-print after the death of both parents. This is said to be in line with the Afrikaner custom as practised in the Transvaal (see Grossman, 1988: 59). Among some English-speaking farmers, the head of the family, upon becoming advanced in age, subdivides his ranch among his children, both male and female, after which he retires leaving the children to manage their farms according to their designs.

The situation is different among the entrepreneurs who run their ranch as a company in which family members are shareholders. According to their practice as observed in the field, the family firm is not usually subdivided among sons after the death of both parents; instead it is kept as one entity in which the heirs continue to be the shareholders. Quite clearly this arrangement, which is followed also by the individualist alternative settler, would do less to encourage the sons to direct their careers into farming than would the Afrikaner arrangement. This partly explains why the individualist English family firm is less able than the familist Afrikaner family firm to involve and retain its sons.

It is important to highlight the link between commoditisation of family labour and the movement of the family firm of the Clarks from one cycle of family development to another. The development of the firm to the stage of a company brings with it the commoditisation of its family labour. Such commoditisation is manifested in one appropriately trained family member taking up the company's management at the going salary rate. By contrast, family labour in Vorster's family firm, which retains its peasant features of familism, remains non-commoditised in the sense that individual family members do not take a salary. In other words, for all its expansion and success, Vorster's family firm remains a family enterprise, avoiding the move to company stage. By the same token, it is the organisational structure of the firm of the Clarks, as seen in its move to the company stage, which triggers the commoditisation of its family labour.

Whereas training on the job is necessary to keep the business going, specialised training is required for successful expansion of the family firm. For that reason, some successful family firms in the western world, where Benedict's study was set, may spend considerable sums of money in training family members. Where sons are neither involved nor trained in the family business, the tendency is that they disperse to other economic activities (Benedict, op. cit.). The settlement in Zimbabwe of the eldest son in the individualist firm may perhaps be explained in the light of this observation. But while trained sons bring new ideas into the business they also want a greater say in how the enterprise is managed. This leads to potential conflict since father and son, belonging to different generations, may not share the same views regarding the management of the enterprise. The formal education of the son may sharpen this difference in views occasioned initially by differences in generation.

To resolve the problem, a compromise has to be reached between the two parties and, for the firm to persist, the father has to give more responsibility to the sons, according to Benedict. Settler firms in the Tuli Block appear to handle the issue of power-sharing between father and sons in a different manner from the one that Benedict posits. The problem of sons demanding more power does not arise in the familist firm because they are fully involved in the firm's management through the process of prestation. In effect, management is shared and decision-making is by consensus, even though the head of the family, by virtue of that position and with all his experience behind him, can be expected to have more say and to decide unilaterally on general issues.

In some respects, the cases of the individualist firm and that of Benson the trader are similar with respect to management. In either case, one son manages on behalf of the rest of the family members who are shareholders. The difference, of course, is that Benson is his father's only son while the individualist firm has two active sons. Since each of the two sons is managing a farm, a comparison could be made between their situation and that of Benson. There is, however, an important point that Benedict makes with respect to western society, but one that is also seen to be applicable in certain instances among Tuli Block settlers. The point concerns the way family enterprises resolve the problem of handling competition for leadership of the family firm between or among the mature sons who are involved full-time in the family enterprise. Benedict notes that in the case of the Rothschild firm that was based in London, a branch had to be opened in Paris, both as a means for the firm to expand and also to give mature sons the opportunity to be managers (Benedict, 1968).

Through keeping farms in South Africa as well as Botswana, Tuli Block settlers seem to be using a similar strategy to avert competition for leadership of the firm among their grown-up sons. The individualist family firm, for example, has another farm in the Transvaal managed by one of its sons. Such a situation takes care of the problem of competition between the firm's two sons.

An explanation of the cohesion of family members of the familist firm and lack of such cohesion in the individualist firm is in order. By cohesion no close friendship or strong natural bond among sons or between them and their parents is implied. The term simply describes a situation in which family members create a social hedge between them as the firm and outsiders. The close-knit family of the familist firm ensures one very crucial concern in family business – the guarding of secrets. Because the family and the business are one and the same thing, business secrets are family secrets

(Benedict, 1968: 5). Family members keep family secrets more tightly than non-family members. The reluctance of members of the familist firm to welcome strangers or freely to discuss general affairs of the firm with non-acquaintances is predicated by the desire to guard all information about the firm. Family members are almost intuitively aware that the manner in which the firm makes money must not be disclosed to outsiders, in case such outsiders be connected to competitors. For various reasons, some of the information relating to the operations of the family firm may be regarded by family members as sensitive.

By contrast to the close-knit family of the familist firm, the more loose-knit individualist firm is welcoming to strangers. Family members discuss the firm's general business affairs more freely with non-acquaintances. This openness, however, does not extend to discussing other family members with strangers. To the extent that business dealings impinge upon the privacy of other family members, they are kept secret.

It can be seen that whereas on the one hand the familist firm shares work among all its family members and is also one coherent family entity, on the other hand the individualist firm does not involve all of its family members. Failure to involve all the family members results in a less cohesive family.

Still, there is a paradox here which needs to be resolved if the mediation of the alternative settler entrepreneurs is to be illuminated further. The paradox is that the familist firm which interacts widely with people is nevertheless seen to keep both strangers and clients away from its inside operations while the individualist firm, which interacts much less with people, is more welcoming to strangers and to people in general. It would appear that the reasons for the contrasting behaviour are different, at least in part. The discussion of bordermanship above brought to light some of the illicit acts of the familist firm. For its illicit dealings, the firm uses its family members, not even its most trusted employees or clients. Its action of keeping all outsiders from the inner structure of its operations can be partly explained by the same argument. It is important that the firm's action of keeping its visitors, who are mostly African, at arm's length is not interpreted simply as practising apartheid.

In the indifference shown by the firm's family members to strangers, there is more than just the fear that secrets will be uncovered. A further look at the situation enables us to appreciate the reason behind the differential response of farmers to extension that is provided by government extensionists. The familist firm does not depend on the state for its extension. Rather, it is generally self-sufficient in this respect, because of its sons whose education has been tailored specifically to suit such needs. If the firm did need some extension service which its sons were unable to provide, it would most probably seek it through its social network in South Africa. In other words, extension can be provided through either the government or social networks.

The familist firm depends almost entirely on social networks while the individualist firm depends for its extension on both the social networks and the government. The farming enterprise of the individualist firm has become integrated into the wider technological and administrative environment while that of the familist firm has remained outside this environment (see also Benvenuti, 1975).

Consequently, the familist firm has less regard for strangers than does the individualist firm whose technocratic manager must always be on the look-out for visitors who may be useful to the firm if they have valuable information and expertise. As a technocrat, he needs that kind of information in order to update his firm, despite his connection with the animal breeding industry in South Africa. He also values chatting with visitors especially those somehow linked with the state. Through such encounters he gets invited by the Ministry of Agriculture to give talks at seminars and perceives that such encounters may further consolidate his position which is dependent on his links with government people.

Hired labour in a family firm

The decision to hire non-family farm labour depends firstly on the developmental cycle reached by the family (Long, 1972: 62) and secondly on the scale of the enterprise (Cheater, 1984: 121). In one sense, the two variables are independent, and scholars emphasise one as the independent variable at the expense of the other, yet in another sense they are interdependent. According to a certain phase in a developmental cycle of the family, work becomes too great to be handled without the assistance of outsiders. When such phases are reached, the scale of the enterprise also warrants hired labour. (Long's and Cheater's views coincide here although elsewhere they differ.)

In discussing the allocation of responsibility in the alternative settler firms, greater detail is given to the familist firm because of greater diversity within its structure. The familist firm depends on African social networks for mediation and also depends on African social contacts for the supply of its permanent and seasonal paid labour. Labour recruitment is channelled along African kinship networks. If a vacancy occurs in any section of the enterprise, be it in merchant trading, cattle herding, fence repairing or elsewhere, in most instances the longest serving employee in that section directs the choice of replacement, recommending one of his own relatives or friends to the paternalist entrepreneur or to his sons. Thus the operational principle is the paternalist one when it comes to defining the relationships between the familist firm and its clients, while the familist principle defines work patterns and role relationships among family members.

To understand the dynamics of labour recruitment and retention of workers, the relationship between the familist and the paternalist principles must be appreciated. The familist firm has no hierarchy or formal positions of authority among its employees, except for the position of foreman. The longest serving employee in each section is in practice the *de facto* head of his section. Possibly no one is designated head of section to avoid demand for higher pay commensurate with the responsibilities of a designated sectional head and yet employees are used as such. Exceptions to this situation are rare. The firm would have a lot to gain by delegating recruitment to the trusted elderly African employees, as recruits feel indebted and show deference to these elderly Africans so that eventually there is harmony and orderliness in the chain of command among the workforce as a whole. This would be a source of strength for the firm. It is the capitalist enterprise that gets stronger because of the deference workers maintain towards elders and because of the mutual support which they give each other according to obligations of kinship which obtain in their social setting outside the farm. The familist firm recognises that its paternalism can only succeed when the people who link the firm with its trading hinterland are content. Because employees recommend their own relatives for vacancies, the labour force is eventually composed of relatives, even though they are of variable closeness to one another.

As a result workers usually perceive themselves to be kin first, workers second. In addition, workers themselves have a sense of 'tradition', derived from their own culture of continuity with life at home, of organising themselves according to received norms of kinship.

What is observed here is actually neo-traditional, That is an achievement of paternalism using a Tswana-derived kinship ideology within a capitalist family firm. Neo-tradition simply refers to a tradition that has been made new or revived. In this case, the Afrikaner settler, also a paternalist entrepreneur, has successfully remodelled the tradition of his African workers in order to exploit its essential features of respect for elders. The nature of the neo-tradition is such that the conversion of kinship for the objectives of the capitalist family firm goes largely unrecognised by the local people themselves. In effect, settler paternalism now harnesses the authority of African elders to the objectives of making profit for the settler firm.

To stress the implications of this argument and other related points about paternalism and neo-tradition it is important to expose flaws in a recent study of farm workers in Botswana by Wylie (1982). Wylie reports on 'insubordination' among young workers on farms owned by the Botswana Livestock Development Corporation (BLDC). But she does not consider the implications of recruitment in an open market. On the BLDC farms, paternalism does not operate. Nor, as a consequence, does the neo-traditional authority of the elders. Failure to recognise the moral importance of the kinship framework in labour recruitment has led Wylie to fail to appreciate one of the reasons for insubordination among younger workers on the Botswana Livestock Development Corporation farms where such a kinship ideology is not used in recruitment. Wylie falls into over-generalised conclusions because she fails to make a series of essential distinctions between the different mediation strategies among the various settler entrepreneurs in the Tuli Block, i.e. the paternalist as opposed to the technocratic entrepreneur, the familist as opposed to the individualist firm, the multi-entrepreneur vis-à-vis the single enterprise (or specialist) farmer.

An important theoretical consideration is the external vis-à-vis the internal types of social relationships in the alternative settler enterprises, which are actually two different farming systems and not just two different types of farms. It is with respect to labour arrangements, both family and hired, that the contrast in the two farming systems emerges. Labour arrangements are tied to the mediation strategies of the firms. Consequently, the opposite principles of familism and individualism which operate with respect to family labour of the firms are a revelation of opposite farming systems at the level of the internal organisation of the two firms. The technocratic and the paternalistic principles which define the external types of social relationships of the alternative firms actually carry the contrast in the farming systems of the two firms beyond the farms to the parties with whom the firms mediate.

Payment levels of hired workers in the familist firm by section

Payment varies by sections of the multiple enterprise, although the question of who recommends a candidate for recruitment also matters.

It is important to clarify what actually are the social origins of the labour force in the familist firm. To do so, the familist firm as a multiple enterprise is considered and the labour force analysed by section. Merchant trading, cattle breeding and fence repairing are of course quite different. Shop assistants need different experience from either cattle herders or fence repairers. It is characteristic of the paternalist entrepreneur that he does not employ already experienced or skilled workers. Rather he chooses to train his own workers with the help of his professionally trained sons. As a result, most workers for the paternalist entrepreneur are not former migrants who have some experience on South African farms, as is the case with workers on some Tuli Block farms, especially the African-owned farms. Provision of on-the-job training seems to contribute to lower turnover of the workers. The paternalist entrepreneur also uses it as an excuse to underpay his workers. His argument is that the cost of training the workers must be recovered from their wages.

Payment in kind varies by section as well, although the trend is reversed, favouring those who are paid the lowest wages. Married cattle herders and fence repairers are each given a 25-kg bag of maize meal per month. Their single counterparts receive half as much maize meal. Unlike on locally owned ranches, herders on settler ranches do not take milk. The reason

TABLE 3.1: Payment levels by section (monthly average).

	Familist firm average	Tuli Block average
Foreman/driver	P180	P120
Shop assistant	P120	P80
Domestic servant	P50	P30
Herder/fence repairer	P20	P15

Source: Author's field data.

given by the settlers for the prohibition is that taking milk is detrimental to the growth rate of calves. Workers see the assured provision of maize meal to be a main attraction of the job as undernourishment is often a problem among their unemployed mates and this benefit actually doubles their pay.

Wylie considers that keeping payment in kind constant over the years suggests that European farmers are aware of the crucial effect of food in retaining the lower paid workers (Wylie, 1982: 413). I would go further and suggest that feeding the herders but showing little concern for their welfare in other respects—consider, for instance, the poor accommodation provided for them—is an indication that settler farmers are interested only in the physical strength of the herders, which they exploit fully. That may be the one reason why farmers prefer to pay more out for maize meal than to increase cash payment. But while all settler ranchers deny the right to take milk, taking milk is a right which most local ranchers uphold. Local ranchers take it for granted that the milk must be shared on the ranch between the herders and the ranch owner as it is in the cattlepost.

A crucial difference between the alternative settler firms is in their recruitment methods. The argument has already been made that the familist firm relies on kinship networks to procure labour. It can be seen from Table 3.2 that in the familist firm, 61 per cent of the entire labour force is hired through social networks while in the individualist firm the corresponding figure is only 25 per cent. Recruitment through social networks has the effect of strengthening the social bonds between the firm and its clients, and tends to protect the firm against labour shortage in rainy months when villagers would want to do the planting of their own crops.

The use of the kinship network in labour recruitment however demands that the firm projects a benevolent attitude in line with the broader norms of paternalism on which it is founded. The firm must be seen to be protective of its labourers and clients at large. Hence, the favours they receive in terms of easy jobs, having their arable fields ploughed for them at cheaper rates, and other forms of easy credit. Through such privileges the firm is trying to create for itself a positive public image. Another advantage of recruiting according to social networks is that despite the low wages paid to workers, the labour turnover is very low.

In the development of the individualist firm, the transformation from cross-border cattle trading to specialist breeding brings with it technocratic management and declining benefits for the workers. The move towards individualism also means that the firm cannot recruit labour in the way that the familist firm does. The individualist firm recruits mainly from the open market and only to a small extent (25 per cent) through social networks. Normally, employment seekers present themselves to the settler farm manager who does his own screening before he can take the decision to hire or not to hire. Occasionally, however, the local foreman recommends job seekers for employment as herders, fence repairers or temporary workers. Usually, such people are either his relatives, or are connected to him in some way. Because the majority of workers in the individualist firm are recruited from the open market and not through family structures, their turnover is higher than in the familist firm, although it is still lower than the turnover of employees on farms owned by locals.

Since the individualist firm specialises mainly in producing exotic cattle breeds, its permanent workers are mainly herders as Table 3.2 shows. For comparable jobs, payment levels are not very different from those in the familist firm:

TABLE 3.2: Methods of labour recruitment: average figures for each type of settler firm.

	Familist firm			Individualist firm		
	A	B	C	A	B	C
Drivers	4	2	50	2	1	50
Shop assistants	5	3	60	0	0	0
Domestic servants	4	3	75	2	0	0
Herders	15	7	47	20	5	25
Fence repairers	10	8	80	12	5	25
Total	38	23	61	36	9	25

A   Number of employees by section.
B   Number of employees hired through social networks.
C   B, as a percentage of A.

Source: Author's data.

In addition to the cash wage, permanent workers in the individualist firm, as in the familist, receive payment in kind, which is 12.5-kg maize meal bag per month for bachelors and 25-kg maize meal bag per month for married workers. Casual employees hired to do piece jobs may be given cooked food but receive no mealie meal.

In general, on most settler ranches, the present trend in net earnings is against the workers.

TABLE 3.3: Monthly payment levels among settler firms.

	Familist firm	Individualist firm	Tuli Block average
Foremen/drivers	P180	P160	P120
Shop assistants	P120	–	P80
Domestic servants	P50	P50	P30
Herders/fencers	P20	P24	P15
Arable workers	P30	–	P25

Source: Author's field data.

CONCLUSION

The concern of this chapter has been an analysis of the factors that have been instrumental in the differential response of the alternative settlers to changes in political and economic opportunity with respect to mediation. Beginning with a distinction between the middleman and settler role, and then relating the distinction to the mediation of the alternative settlers, the chapter has given an account of the change to specialisation in the individualist firm and the continuation, as well as the enhancement, of multiple enterprise in the familist firm. It was emphasised that the organisation of family labour has been the pervasive factor in triggering the difference in strategy each firm has adopted. In a situation where sons remain within the firm, expansion is easily achieved through engagement in multiple enterprise. A settler firm that does not have many sons in it may expand, but, as the profiles of Benson and Mulder have shown, it has to employ a European manager or otherwise switch to specialised production, an activity that can be managed with a single hand.

The process through which sons are made to develop an enduring interest in the family enterprise has been analysed. Even though prestation can explain the two-fold process of the way a firm expands on the basis of trust and confidence and how it incorporates sons, it still does not provide an adequate explanation because it takes more than just the prestation to co-opt and retain sons in the family firm. The scale of the enterprise has been seen to be significant because for sons to stay within the firm, they need to see in it a bright future for themselves.

The role of the state has been seen to be significant in the enterprises of some but not all settlers. While the impact of the state in the success of the enterprises of some settlers cannot be denied, it emerged quite clearly that some of the most successful settler entrepreneurs are not directly backed by the state. Settler entrepreneurs without such direct backing have evolved their own information systems through social networks with their kin and business associates across the national frontier. Those of them whose enterprises overtly depend on the state use both the state and their social networks across the border for extension services.

A direct result of using different sources of extension services is the differential response to outsiders by the alternative firms. A firm which depends on its own social resources for extension services is less welcoming to strangers while one that depends on the state for the service tends to be more welcoming. Differences in lifestyles as in attitudes towards strangers, are best interpreted within the frame of mediation, and not independently of it. Whatever the behaviour of the entrepreneurs, the aim is always to further the interests of the enterprise.

Allowing for that, the entrepreneurial infrastructure that is developed outside the state seems to be more viable and more stable than that which is developed within the framework of the state.

Closely associated with the organisational resources of settler mediation has been what I have called 'bordermanship'. The analysis of the mediation of the familist firm has illuminated the force of bringing together both sides of the national frontier in the Tuli Block. Through careful management of the resources which straddle the national frontier, such as the Limpopo river, or farms and families, the Afrikaners have been able to expand their enterprises more than those of the English entrepreneurs, who have lacked such resources. The concept of bordermanship also helps explain the differences in the lifestyles of the settlers. Settlers that have wider social links with the Transvaal have a tendency to live a lifestyle that is consistent with their entrepreneurial success, whereas those with narrower social links tend to live more private lives which do not display their level of success.

Another factor that has been central to the success and expansion of the familist firm is the manner in which the firm harnesses the local community to provide the whole range of its entrepreneurial requirements. Such requirements include labour; the source of production goods, namely the cattle and goats; and a market for its merchandise. In order for it to obtain this benefit from the local community, the firm develops paternalism, a strategy that creates an outward image of security for its clientele, while in effect it gives the firm an undue advantage in its trade dealings with its clientele. For example, paternalism enables the entrepreneur to exploit the kinship tradition of deference for elders for the purpose of serving his capitalist firm. In the process, he is able to extract from the labour resources of the community use value and not the exchange value. In this way, the capitalist enterprise is able to make considerable profit because the labour is very much underpaid.

For general trading between the entrepreneur and the local community, barter is used as a medium of exchange. Although on the surface the price of items of trade is set jointly by the entrepreneur and the community, the sharp inequality in terms of economic strength between the two parties has the effect of virtually giving the entrepreneur a monopoly in the setting of the price. Effectively, the local community is a captive market for the entrepreneur.

Yet the clientele do not resign themselves to their situation. They counteract the moves of the entrepreneur by forging links with the rest of the country through their children who take up jobs in towns or set up small businesses there. The local community does not attempt to break its ties with the paternalist entrepreneur; they are aware of the benefits of the bond between them and him, in spite of overall exploitation. In developing contacts with the outside they simply want to increase their alternatives for survival.

4

PROFILES OF LOCAL ENTREPRENEURS

The history of early European settlement in the Tuli Block up to the opening of the abattoir in 1956 shows that the early settlers were mainly from less well-off families, mostly poor farmers from the Transvaal. The exceptions were the English settlers who were relatively better off than the Afrikaner. By the 1980s, however, virtually all the settlers may be said to have attained elite status. On the other hand, the locals who have bought Tuli Block ranches after Botswana's independence in 1966, already were, with a few exceptions, elites, not by settler standards, but by their own village standards. Most of them were large-scale cattle farmers, with the exception of a few non-elite.

There are other differences between them and their fellow settler entrepreneurs. Whereas the expansion of settler enterprise is based on the farm, that of local farmers is based in the communal areas, from where they merely expand into freehold farms. And while the settlers did not have grazing rights in the communal areas until after independence, local farmers who expanded into freehold areas have retained their grazing rights in the communal areas, thus giving them an advantage in terms of searching for pasture between the two places when cordon fences have not prevented it.

Although the expansion of the local farmers into the Tuli Block took place against the background of growing land scarcity and within the general tide of land privatisation following the commercialisation of cattle production, to say that the reason for buying a farm is simply to make a living is simplistic and may not be the primary aim of those who are members of the elite (see also Cheater, 1984), for the elite discern that land is being commoditised in the process of state formation during the post-colonial era. It is, of course, not so wrong or simplistic when said about the early Tuli Block settlers, who were generally poor. After all, the early settlers, even if also traders, were farmers; they had no livelihood that was not in any way integrated with farming.

However, members of the district or national elite, especially civil servants and traders, are hard to categorise as farmers (see also Parson, 1979). While recognising the relationship between farming operations and their other economic pursuits, it is not always easy to map the exact nature and form of that relationship. As Cheater correctly points out in her study of Msengezi farmers, the reasons for purchasing farms are various and they cannot always be put in terms of a simple rationality of income. The overriding reason, to give an example, may be to provide security for a future retirement, so that there may be no concern about immediate profits (Cheater, 1984: 98).

Similar observations have been made elsewhere about farmers' diverse intentions in farm ownership. In the Plains of North America, early settlers around 1900 were heterogeneous in their backgrounds and in their reasons for buying farms. Some of them merely wanted to subsist, while others wanted to get rich quick (Bennett, 1979: 214). Another instance but without bearing on the Tuli Block as far as I have observed, is in the Seychelles where land ownership means status, even if it yields nothing (Benedict and Benedict, 1982: 186). In the Tuli Block, it would be a mistake to dismiss the interest in the yield, at least from the viewpoint of elites. What must be appreciated, however, is the great weight given to considerations of status in elite decisions about ranch purchase and, thus, about the yield. Such status considerations weigh heavily, in particular, when the member of the elite is also of royal descent as shown in the profile of Kgari. Another consideration for local farmers in buying a Tuli Block farm might be the shortage of grazing land in the western sandveld, the highly productive and exclusive traditional place for large-scale cattle producers in the communal areas since before independence. Gulbrandsen reports that for some time it has become increasingly difficult for farmers to obtain a cattle-grazing site in this part of the country (Gulbrandsen, 1984: 114).

Considering further that moving to the western sandveld, if a grazing site could be found, would require sinking a borehole, and that the cost of sinking and equipping the borehole would be equal to the price of 500 hectares in the freehold areas, most local farmers who wanted to expand their herds might have opted for an outright purchase of a freehold farm. Lack of knowledge about conventional ranching in general and the capacity of the farm in particular, might have induced locals to go ahead and buy farms without sufficient consideration. A number of them overestimate the capacity of their small farms. In part, such overestimation may be predicated by government extension which alleges that profit margins can be more than doubled on fenced ranches (Botswana Government White Paper No. 2 of 1975).

Contrary to the government's assertion, Hitchcock alleges that statistics from the Nojane ranches which were developed and fenced by the state through a Swedish International Development Authority (SIDA) loan in western Botswana show that calving rates, which are considered to be very important productivity indicators in cattle farming, are actually lower than those for cattleposts. In 1978, Hitchcock's figures of calving rates were 7 per cent for the ranches and between 14 per cent and 18 per cent for the cattleposts (Hitchcock, 1978: 300–1). Government researchers had put the calving rate for cattleposts at a very low level of between 3 per cent and 3.5 per cent.

It is clear that the state is behind the privatisation of farm land or the move to ranches, and behind the state are people, the elites. In spite of this, the general point to stress is that the reasons for ranching or simply for ranch ownership cannot be taken for granted without the risk of misinterpreting ranchers' intentions and purposes. Even more important: it is easy to say that ranching *is* what ranchers *do*, but we cannot assume from the appearance of beef for the market that we know what ranching is for the rancher. To say what ranching is, we have to know, above all, who the *rancher* is. And to know that, in the Tuli Block, we have to analyse the external relations of ranchers when they mediate with others as well as the internal ones among themselves. In other words, we have to map the farming system of each entrepreneur through labour and other social and institutional arrangements that are involved in the production of value or commodity. This is the approach that social analysis takes in this chapter.

The problem of undercapitalisation is one that the settlers have overcome by building their ranches piecemeal over time. Slowly, the settlers gained the necessary experience to live on the farms and also to make farming a profitable occupation by linking it with ancillary economic activities or, eventually, by specialisation in exotic breeds. On the other hand, the local ranchers, most of whom are not resident on the farms, have still to come to grips with conventional ranching. They do not fully understand ranch life and lack of such vital knowledge is reflected in their poorly planned attempts to produce exotic breeds.

Most importantly, however, understanding ranch life and practising conventional ranching is not their concern. Their major aim is to develop their total economy and not their farms *per se*. It has to be understood that the total economy of the ranchers includes the cattlepost and any other economic activities that they may be involved in. The 'development' that the locals envisage is therefore complex, yet it has the effect of increasing cattle herds, improved through the use of exotic bulls, and with minimum financial input in production.

Hence their failure to develop their farms through the construction of paddocks or renovating farm houses as well as their use of unskilled cheap labour. More about the use of untrained labour is presented before the profiles of these local entrepreneurs. Meantime use of the term *undercapitalised* in reference to the farming enterprises of local farmers has to be somewhat guarded. A number have many cattle some of which they could sell in order to raise whatever capital was needed for a more conventional kind of ranching, loan repayment or whatever and, in a number of instances, it is by choice that their farming operations remain seemingly undercapitalised.

Scholars have generally missed this crucial point about local farmers. For that reason, a number of them have often unduly castigated the farmers for taking very expensive options such as producing exotic breeds with neither adequate costing nor preparation for their marketing. Equally, scholars have wrongly interpreted the action of local farmers to obtain big loans at interest rates higher than the internal rate of return of the ranches as a failure on the part of farmers to understand finance, and converting the farm into some kind of cattlepost as merely a sign that farmers have not understood conventional ranching. The claim that local farmers lack a full understanding of conventional ranching is generally true. But what is more important is that they are fighting against the ranch-oriented policies of the state because their own cattle production system requires the integration of the ranch and the cattlepost. This applies as much to the non-elites who are not involved in the formulation of state policies as to the elites who are behind the movement from communal areas to ranches. It is important for all of them to strategise in this way so that they can avert the risks from frequent droughts.

This is not to suggest that by devising their own ranching system the local farmers have solved all their problems. As is evident from the profiles that follow, a spiral of contradictory processes is still discernible even as they operationalise their self-devised farming systems. For example, there are a number of instances when their ranching enterprises are clearly under economic strain. That may partly be due to drought; but inappropriate ranching strategies and the mismanagement of the overall economic activities of the farmer cannot be ruled out.

An accusation that seems to have been rightly made about local freehold farmers is that they have bought farms that are too small and most of which lack a river frontage. Table A.1a shows that the farms of the locals in the Tuli Block are much smaller than those of settlers. Many locals buy paddocks or 'camps' on farms formerly owned by settlers. The Table shows that the average size of a farm owned by a local is 2,152 hectares, while a settler owns an average of 7,739 ha. if he is an Afrikaner, or 6,842 ha. if he is English. This means that on average a local owns about one-third of the land held by a settler of English origin or a quarter of the land held by an Afrikaner farmer.

To give an account of the transfer of land from the settlers to the locals, one must go back a little into the history of the Tuli Block. Between 1956 when the Lobatse abattoir was opened and 1966 when Botswana gained its independence some settlers from the Tuli Block returned to South Africa. They sold their farms. To make the sale easier, the settlers subdivided their ranches into smaller units which would each cost less than the whole farm. Whereas all farms had river frontage while they were still owned by the settlers, the action of sub-dividing them has left certain portions without river frontage (cf. Figures 1.3 and 1.4). Local farmers who have bought those farms without river frontage have been forced to sink boreholes on their newly-acquired smaller farms and this has made their ranching costlier than that of the settlers.

At first sight these instances seem to question the wisdom of the local farmers moving from communal cattle-raising to ranches. However, the picture becomes quite different once the connection between the farm and the cattlepost is brought in to view. It is arguable that even more fundamental to the movement of locals into freehold areas is the development pattern that is being charted by the emergent post-colonial state. In Botswana, as in many other developing countries which follow a free enterprise development model, the state is covertly or overtly implementing a land commercialisation programme. According to Vandergeest,

> the state is not only an agent of commoditisation, the process of state formation is part and parcel of commoditisation and the twin process of economic commoditisation and political state formation cannot be understood apart from one another when treated from a long term historical point of view. (Vandergeest, 1988: 16)

Large-scale farmers, that is the elite, some of whom are in the state mechanism, see the trend towards the commoditisation of land more clearly than do the small cattle farmers who are not always in a position to view the growing land scarcity within the broad context of the pattern of national development. As Heijdra rightly advises, it is crucial to keep the totality of the processes in mind because farmers do many interconnected things simultaneously (Heijdra, 1989: 97). Once the interconnection emerges, it is seen that in spite of the loss-making appearance of the farms of the locals, the same farmers are able to achieve their primary ambition.

Nor is their primary ambition simple and straightforward. It is complicated by the fact that it is not uniform across the categories of either the district elite or the national elite. At the centre of the complication is the use into which the farm is put. The way the farm is used by different farmers seems to be more or less the same. As such, it does not easily help us understand the reason for its acquisition. For instance, the aim of increasing the size of the herds is not only a common one across the categories and among local farmers in general; it is also a consequence of the integration of the cattlepost and the farm, something that is practised by almost all local farmers.

Nevertheless, there are some discernible variations in the use of the farm, even though such variations still do not assist us much to fathom the reason for buying the farm. For some local entrepreneurs, it can be seen more clearly within the broader picture of their cattle farming activities that the farm is used mainly, though not solely, for producing exotic breeds while the cattlepost is used mainly for producing indigenous breeds. It is more convenient for farmers to organise their production that way because the western sandveld as a free range exposes cattle to the risk of theft and is not as well-equipped as the farm to produce exotic breeds which need more care than the hardy indigenous breeds. For that reason, and also, of course, because there is clearly more to freehold ranch ownership than mere production of cattle, the Tuli Block remains indispensable to local elites.

A related point is that variations in the use of the farm, i.e. various types of farms, are not the same as various types of farming enterprises. Various types of farms can indeed be based on the same type of farming enterprise. I have indicated in Chapter 1 that a farming system (which is synonymous with a farming enterprise) is socially, institutionally and geographically defined. On the other hand, a type of farm cannot be defined in similar terms.

The final point before the profiles of the local ranchers concerns labour. When the Nojane farms which were referred to earlier were demarcated, the government took the trouble to train a number of people as ranch assistants at the Ramatlabama Livestock Development Centre, in the southern part of the country. The government had expected that the ranch assistants would be hired by the farmers in the Nojane ranches. However, the farmers kept their herders from the cattleposts and did not employ any of the trained ranch assistants. According to Hitchcock, the Nojane farmers did not hire the trained ranch assistants because they were afraid that trained workers would demand higher wages than those paid to normal cattlepost herders (Hitchcock, 1982: 18).

The situation in the Tuli Block is no different from that of Nojane. On their farms local farmers use their herders from the cattleposts. While Hitchcock may be correct in that financial considerations are central to the use of cattlepost labour on farms, other factors are also involved. The labour process is essentially a craft. Farmers perceive that a farm worker who has received formal training may not necessarily be more productive than one who has been trained on the job. A comparison of workers on settler farms with those on the state-owned Botswana Livestock Development Corporation (BLDC) farms in terms of quality of labour shows that workers on settler farms, in spite of their lack of formal education, are much more experienced and more productive than their formally-educated counterparts on BLDC farms (Mazonde, 1987). In addition farmers, wanting to control the labour process that is involved in their enterprises, wish to be independent of the state or any outside agency in the supply of their labour.

In fact, Nojane farmers may have perceived the training of ranch assistants by the state as some kind of commoditisation and institutionalisation of the labour process which is usually a result of direct intervention by the state and agribusiness in a situation of increasing incorporation of firms into markets (see van der Ploeg, 1990: 268). Farmers resist such measures because they take away the labour process from their control. As indicated above, issues of ranching, including the question of labour, have to be taken within the broader context of the entire mediation of the farmers.

PROFILES OF LOCAL ENTREPRENEURS
Tau – the upwardly mobile entrepreneur

Tau exemplifies the possibility of social mobility, climbing out of a relatively low social position through saving and careful investment of money earned from labour migration. This case also highlights the dilemmas and predicaments in the making of a capitalist family firm out of a non-capitalist one, beginning with speculation and marketing in the communal areas and moving on to production in the commercial ranches. A point about Tau is that he was observed by another social scientist during his heyday in the communal areas, around 1976, before he entered the Tuli Block (see 'Samson' in Mahoney, 1977: 300–6). Then, his activities were different from those observed during 1985–90 when, in his economic decline, he had been forced out of his major revenue-earning activity, speculation, by competition and drought. Tau's career and the careers of other local ranchers in this study, must be seen against the twenty-year drought cycle which has become characteristic of Botswana (see Tyson, 1978: 10).

Observations were made when these ranchers were at a low point in the drought cycle. Rains have improved since 1986 when the initial fieldwork ended. The discontinuation in 1990 of the arable lands development programme, a state initiative meant to help farmers recover from the drought, suggests that the government considers that farmers have had sufficient time and assistance to recover from the drought of the 1980s. In spite of this view, some freehold farmers seem to have suffered irretrievable damage to their farming enterprises, so that even in the period following the improved rains, their ranching enterprises, if still owned, are seen to suffer from the effects of the drought.

Of course the drought factor, important as it is in contributing to the hardship that is being faced by the ranchers in the Tuli Block as well as in other areas of the country, must not be projected as if it is their only problem. As the case of Tau shows, local farmers especially, also have socio-behaviourial problems as well.

Tau is in his mid-fifties. His formal education stopped after he completed primary school. Together with his two sisters Tau had inherited nothing from his father who had been poor, though respected for his position in the church. To enter business he had had to use earnings accumulated in South Africa where he worked as a policeman for some ten years.

Mahoney, in his study of the home village of Tau, suggests that small traders always remained small and never make it into the category of large traders (see Mahoney, 1977: 323). Contrary to that assertion, his large trader, Samson (Tau) did just that, hence, he is referred to as the upwardly-mobile entrepreneur. The drought of 1971–3 which was accompanied by the outbreak of foot-and-mouth disease provided Tau with the opportunity to enter into cattle speculation, the activity which revolutionised his economic activities and for a time made him the most prosperous cattle dealer in his sub-district. This was, for Tau, a definite breakthrough: from a small trader specialising in food-retailing (butchery and a restaurant) to a larger trader dealing in cattle as well. In line with standing veterinary rules and regulations, the outbreak of foot-and-mouth disease was followed by an embargo on cattle movement across veterinary cordon fences. As a result, a great number of cattle accumulated in cattle posts during the eighteen-month period of the outbreak of foot-and-mouth disease.

In 1972, as soon as the foot-and-mouth outbreak was cleared, restrictions on cattle movement were lifted. Tau acted fast. Noticing people's desperate need to market their animals and the inadequate marketing channels in the area (at the time, the settlers from the Tuli Block were the main cattle buyers) he seized the opportunity and entered into cattle speculation, purchasing from producers in his sub-district and selling to the abattoir, through a cattle agency which he started for that purpose (see Mahoney, 1977: 300–6 for a fuller account).

The settler ranchers from the Tuli Block had for many years formed a formidable cordon of cattle buyers, keeping Africans out of the cattle business. Tau was able to penetrate this cordon in a very interesting manner. He paid more for the cattle than did the settlers, yet less than the BMC prices. Of course, the settlers were paying very low prices both in cash and through barter as already shown in Chapter 2. Tau was seen by the people as their rescuer from settler avarice and was in this way able to capture the cattle market from some of the settlers, especially those that did not tie debt to credit as indicated in previous chapters. However, he avoided competition with Vorster, whom he regarded as his mentor. Whereas Vorster specialised in buying unfinished stock, which were cheaper to buy and which he would finish equally cheaply on his large farm, Tau, who had no farm at this time, concentrated on the more expensive finished stock which he sent to the BMC abattoir as quickly as he obtained the quota for selling animals.

The pricing policy of the BMC, and thus the state policy at the time, gave a boost to Tau's venture. It was the policy of the abattoir to pay low prices to cattle producers at the time of slaughter and to give a bonus at the end of the abattoir's financial year. Roughly, the producer received two-thirds of the full price of the beast when selling, and a further one-third as bonus (Botswana Government, 1977: 16). This arrangement placed Tau at an advantage because his low profit margin during the year, occasioned by his relatively high cattle-purchase prices, was compensated for at the end of the year when he received his bonus. In 1973, after only eighteen months in cattle speculation, he received a remarkable P90,000 (£20,000) as bonus.

A bonus of this magnitude was not common among local traders and it struck everybody including Vorster. Tau publicised it far and wide and in the process his own fame spread like wild fire. With his P90,000 in hand, the upwardly mobile entrepreneur felt that the time had come for him to take one rung up the ladder of elitism and enter into commercial land. He used part of that money to pay the deposit which then qualified him for a National Development Bank loan with which he bought a 637-ha. farm, adjacent to Vorster's large farm on the western side of the Tuli Block. Tau's farm does not have a river frontage or direct access from the Tuli Block frontline road. This farm, together with the farms of Pitso and Molema, were originally owned by a settler who had kept them as three separate farms, each with its own house, an unusual situation for adjacent farms belonging to the same person in the Tuli Block, the tendency being for adjacent farms owned by the same person to have a house built on only one of them. However, some farmers had already purchased adjacent farms which had farm houses on each (see for example, the Clarks' farm). The fact that each of the three adjacent farms owned by the local ranchers (Tau, Molema, Pitso – all of them discussed in this study) has its own settler-type house, strongly suggests that the farms might have come under different ownership over time, so that their last settler owner was not their original owner. With respect to Tau, the most important thing justifying his claim as an elite is that he was the first local from his sub-district to buy a freehold farm.

But whereas Tau had been successful in organising himself to seize economic opportunities and expand within a very short time, he was not so successful in organising other people, or his labour. The organisation of labour on his multiple enterprise has been fraught with problems, which in part stemmed from his own abuse of trust. Lacking grown-up sons to help him in ways his two grown-up daughters could not, he made up for the shortage of nuclear family labour in various ways. One way was to co-opt an unemployed son of a cousin who worked as his general assistant, supervising the restaurant and the butchery in the village, once he had purchased the farm. (I do not have the socio-demographic characteristics of his employees in the restaurant and butchery.) Around 1979, Tau bought a butchery in a nearby town and employed his son-in-law to run it for him.

The arable farming activities on his newly acquired farm reveals both another way in which he obviated the problem of lack of sons and yet abused the trust of people who might have helped him further to greater economic heights. The year 1974 was a rainy one for his part of the Tuli Block. On his farm he had been grazing the trade cattle for which he had not obtained BMC marketing quotas. Even so, land was still available on his farm for arable production. Tau decided to produce groundnuts, a crop that had an attractive market across the border in the Transvaal (see Vorster's profile, especially his son, Verlem). But in spite of his rapid economic success, Tau had not yet acquired farming implements by the time he contemplated the idea of producing groundnuts in 1974. Nor did he have the money on hand to purchase a tractor and farming implements.

Consequently, he entered into an informal agreement with a man from another village near his farm, who had a tractor and sufficient funds to purchase groundnut seeds and the diesel for ploughing. The agreement was that they would share the profits of the crop equally. In this mutual agreement, Tau's only contribution was the land on the farm. The harvest was excellent. A total of 1,300 bags of crop were harvested and marketed in the Transvaal, where they fetched P32,000, an amount that was P4,000 above the cost of the farm when it was bought the previous year. Despite efforts to claim a share, the villager got nothing from Tau and the partnership immediately ceased. Since that year, Tau has not planted anything on that farm.

In pursuit of an expanded enterprise and also perhaps having seen what honour his first ranch had brought him, Tau purchased yet another farm, using part of the profit from the cash crop as a deposit. He signed another National Development Bank mortgage and completed the transaction in 1977. The second farm, measuring 3,000 ha., was not adjacent to the first one, but was completely separated from it by a portion of Vorster's ranch, having been part of a farm that had been deliberately partitioned to make its sale easier. Hence, there was no house on it. By buying a farm that was not adjacent to the first one, Tau betrayed his lack of foresight regarding the economics of management.

By contrast, the better-experienced settler ranchers expanded their land as a single unit (cf. Vorster and the Clarks). Most probably, however, Tau was inspired by the African mentality which finds greatness, not in the amount of land or size of ranch, but rather in the quantity of farms, notwithstanding their sizes. In his home village, people used to talk of him as the man with two Tuli Block farms. Among settlers, the reverse is true; grandeur is based on the size of a ranch and not necessarily on the quantity of farms.

After buying the second farm, Tau made an attempt to buy a third, but this time he did not succeed as he had clearly reached the peak of his expansion and was at the beginning of his steady decline. Since 1973 when he bought his first ranch, the state policy, which had created an opportunity for him to break into successful cattle trading, was gradually changing for the worse for him and for most other speculators. The state decided to promote the Agriculture and Marketing Co-operatives which it set up specifically to increase cattle marketing in the rural areas, where hitherto the marketing channel had been provided almost solely by speculators and cattle agencies. The entry of the Agriculture and Marketing Co-operative in Tau's sub-district increased the number of cattle marketing channels to three, besides the private sales between friends, neighbours and fellow villagers. First were the speculators who simply bought cattle from producers, mostly from kraals and public sales yards on official marketing days. They were the most notorious of all buyers because they paid the lowest prices. It had been from such speculators, who were mostly settlers, that Tau had been regarded as a rescuer by cattle producers in his home district. Second were the cattle agencies who sold cattle to the BMC and only withheld 2½ per cent of the BMC price, passing the rest of it on, less the railway haulage charges and government taxes, to the producer. These were regarded more highly than the speculators but producers were still not quite satisfied with them because they did not pass on the bonus, about one-third of the cost of an animal, to the producer. Tau had made his wealth in these two ways, as speculator and as owner of a cattle-selling agency.

Third came the Agriculture and Marketing Co-operative and it charged not the 2½ per cent commission of the price of each and every beast it sold to the BMC on behalf of the customer, but twice as much, 5 per cent. On the other hand it did not withhold the bonus; the co-operative, as it is commonly called, remitted it to the customer as soon as BMC made such bonus available. For members of the co-operative there was an added advantage. Members received a dividend or share of the profit, if the co-operative movement made a profit at the end of the year.

Although it would seem that the co-operative easily undercut the speculators and the agencies, there were social ties binding the agencies and the speculators to the cattle producers, as I have already stated. For that reason, the state fought long and hard to win the rural producers to the side of the co-operative, and it was not until around 1978 that the co-operative had an edge over the other marketing channels (see Parson, 1979: 292). Despite the tough battle that the state waged with other cattle buyers, its action nevertheless constituted a major challenge to Tau's entrepreneurship. Worst affected was his role as a speculator, the very role that had been crucial in helping him economically. Second, the state dealt Tau another decisive blow in his role as cattle agent, the only role then sustaining him in the cattle industry after losing his place amongst speculators. In 1975, the state changed its pricing policy of splitting payment between two-thirds of the price of the beast on the date of purchase of cattle and a further one-third afterwards as bonus. The abattoir was directed to pay the complete value of the beast upon purchasing it. This was because it had been observed that a bonus arrangement benefited speculators and agencies unfairly, and was disadvantageous to cattle producers who fell victims to such speculators and agencies through inescapable social ties (cf. Vorster's and Benson's mediation for example). These changes in state policy put Tau in a serious dilemma. Before long, a long term of drought aggravated his predicament and left him an impoverished man.

To get out of his dilemma, he tried, unsuccessfully, to switch over to exotic breeding on his two farms. Then, as now, it was regarded as prestigious to produce pure breeds, especially on freehold farms. Tau sought to connect more effectively the commercial and the communal areas through exotic breeds in the way the Clarks did. In his case, however, a major obstacle was that he lacked both the financial and the state backing for this risky and very expensive undertaking. With the drought just beginning, the odds were clearly set firmly against him.

In 1978, despite the economic problems that were besetting him, Tau's social credit was still strong and he was lent P10,000 by a commercial bank in order to buy breeding stock from South Africa. No sooner had he bought his three bullocks and fifteen heifers, all of them pure brahmans, than a major drought period, to which I have already referred, began all over southern Africa.

In north-eastern Botswana, of which Tau's farms are a part, the severity of the drought was aggravated by the outbreak of foot-and-mouth disease which prompted the restrictions on cattle movement outside of the Tuli Block. Restrictions on cattle movement meant that Tau could neither carry out his cattle-agency business in the communal areas, nor could he market whatever breeds he was able to produce on his Tuli Block farms. Without the state support which those who are linked directly with the state through the type of contract that the Clarks had, he could not market his few exotic weaners during periods of restrictions on cattle movement. Such restrictions were lifted intermittently, but never in a way that could sufficiently help people in Tau's position.

The effect of all this was that Tau's venture into breeding did not provide the escape that it had been meant to provide, namely, the escape from the dilemma he was facing in the marketing business of trade cattle. He ran short of cash on almost each of his multiple enterprises. As the drought persisted, his two butcheries gradually suffered a decline: slaughter animals slowly became scarce and eventually, Tau was forced to slaughter cattle from his own cattlepost, located within the sub-districts for his butcheries. At this time, certain settler entrepreneurs who found themselves trapped inside the cordon fences for the supply of cattle for sale in their butcheries, were forced to depend for their meat supply solely upon their Tuli Block farms. But unlike them, Tau depended on the communal areas for his butchery's cattle supply. His two butcheries, one in a village and the other in a town, and the sources of his cattle supply, were both in the same veterinary cordon area so that his meat-retailing business was not as much affected by cattle movement restriction as was that of the settler entrepreneurs in question.

However, that position has changed since the mid-1980s, when, due to scarcity of slaughter cattle in the communal areas, Tau has been forced to slaughter, much against his will, improved cattle from his farms, for his butcheries. His major aim in embarking upon the improvement of his cattle breeds, he explained, had been to be the first local to rise to the level of the Clarks, a level he openly envied.

In summary then, Tau's ranching enterprise has failed to expand. As indicated in the introduction to this profile, his failure is not only due to changes in state policy and the drought, but equally to his abuse of trust in his dealings with business associates. Having outlined the other reasons behind his entrepreneurial failure, that is, drought and changes in state policies, his abuse of trust, which emerged during his dealings with his partner in producing groundnuts on the farm is now considered.

In order to explain Tau's conduct in this partnership, an account of his whole tactic in business dealings is called for. Tau realises that for a large trader such as himself, a good reputation is indispensable. That reputation is built upon public and not personal activities carried out in private. As Mahoney rightly puts it, 'for large traders, such public activities are not interpersonal dealings but consist in community images' (Mahoney, 1977: 263). For instance, the fact that Tau is credited by villagers with being solely responsible for the high level of livestock prices in his home area, gives him the image of someone who has the common good of others at heart. Mahoney goes on to state that in the days of his prosperity, Tau refrained as much as possible from interpersonal dealings with customers, including participation in open competition with other villagers for the many elected Farmers' Day Association officers 'in which details of behaviour would become public knowledge' (Mahoney, 1977: 263).

From Mahoney's account, it is clear that Tau preferred grand gestures (that is, 'big man' image-making ventures) such as sponsoring a local football team, donating to Independence Day celebrations (for which he received public acknowledgement), and taking an honorary and non-competitive post, such as a nominated president, rather than an elected chairman, of the Farmers' Day Association. He then came to the kraal to trade with a reputation which was widespread and based on his dedication to the communal good, says Mahoney, op. cit. Interestingly enough, Mahoney cites an incident in which he witnessed a crack appear in Tau's public image (Mahoney, 1977: 265–6). On that occasion, an old man came along to the public kraal and waited till a large crowd had gathered before he shouted at the top of his voice, accusing Tau of denying that he (the old man) had delivered a beast to him (Tau) for which no payment was given.

What Mahoney seems to have failed to notice was that the incident of the old man was only the tip of the iceberg of negative features of Tau's character which were masked by his 'big man' image. Put together with his conduct in his partnership with the man who planted groundnuts on his farm, the old man's incident becomes very important in understanding the real character

of Tau. The two incidents indicate that Tau's reputation as a village bene-
factor, which appeared to subsume the important understanding that he is
an honest trader, hid negative aspects to his character, particularly abuse of
trust.

It is interesting to compare Tau's perception of his current state of economic
performance with that of his observers, including his fellow villagers and
traders. In the comparison his real character emerges as well as his self-
aggrandising entrepreneurial tactics.

The general feeling in Tau's village, in the small villages adjacent to his
Tuli Block farms and amongst the settlers who know him and have worked
with him such as Charles, Vorster and Benson, is that his entrepreneurial
career, especially as a 'big man', is over. Vorster, who knows Tau better
than any other settler, considers that Tau deliberately bought his two farms
at very high prices for prestigious reasons. Considering that Tau bought 637
hectares for P28,000 in 1973, paying P40 per hectare, when the ruling price
only became that much (P40 per ha.) in 1980, one is inclined to agree with
Vorster. Vorster's estimate is that the land was worth P18 per hectare at the
time, that is, less than half of what Tau paid for it.

There is, of course, the question of the ability to bargain. Certainly, with
his many years in the Tuli Block, all of his life on the farms and his
considerable wealth which gives him clout, Vorster bargains much more
effectively than Tau. Vorster considers that Tau and Molema, both of
whom he regards as having paid a status price for their farms, will find it
very difficult to repay their loans whose interest rates he believes to be
much higher than the internal rate of return of each of the two farms. The
settler also believes that Tau's two farms are under-utilised, not because
they have very few herds, but because Tau does not take advantage of
available rains which are enough to produce a crop in a rainy season, as
Vorster himself does.

Vorster also considers that Tau was very careless with his money while he
had it. Referring to the P90,000 bonus that Tau received around 1974,
Vorster exclaims 'what he did with all that money I don't know!'. Benson,
who pays less for his cattle through barter, considers that Tau's bankruptcy
was inevitable so long as he continued to pay the high prices he paid for his
trade cattle. Charles dismisses Tau as a prestige seeker who went bust in the
course of his efforts to impress the public. These views are generally shared
by villagers in the sub-district.

Yet for his own part, Tau is still trying hard to present himself as the
successful entrepreneur of his heyday to those who do not know him. He
boasts of his bulls which he claims to be pure-bred, when, in actual fact,
most of them are crosses or hybrids of exotic bulls with indigenous cows.
An all-round economic loss is forcing him to sell his restaurant and the town
butchery. Rather than accept this anticipated sale as a sign of economic

decline, he prefers to view it as a move from multiple enterprise to specialising in breeding. He concedes that the restaurant and the butchery have not been making money since the drought started, but he gives the impression that his ranches are currently profitable, as he is able to barter his bulls with indigenous cattle at the rate of one exotic bull to eight indigenous cattle. The fact is, however, that such exchange occurs very rarely, and irregularly, so much so that for a long time he has been pestering the Ministry of Agriculture, without any success, for a state contract to supply the state with bulls.

During the eighteen months of initial field work, only two exchanges of bulls with traditional herds were witnessed, both of which took place in Tau's home village. The agreements were made in Tau's kraal outside his large house but the actual transactions took place at his cattlepost. On the ranches, his herders state that he has not sold many bulls in recent years. Apparently, the fear that the drought has not completely broken has reduced the demand for bulls among communal area producers. Tau has not been successful in a bid to obtain a state contract to supply exotic bulls because, on the basis of his production standards, the government considers him uncompetitive. He is not the only local cattle producer who has been refused such a state contract.

A public event which boosts Tau's morale and which still gives him an ostensible reason to refuse to acknowledge that he has lost his superiority in the livestock business, is the Agriculture and Trade Fair which is held annually in his and other large villages of the country, culminating in a larger show in the national capital. The fair attracts a lot of public attention and draws large crowds. Ever since Tau started to produce exotic breeds from around 1979, he has been winning the best prize for exotic breeds in his home village. For one reason or another, very few settlers participate in the show. Probably, the settlers do not participate in the village show because they do not regard themselves as part of the local community. The large sitting-room of Tau's house, in which he lives with his first wife, is bedecked with 'Champion of the Yard' prizes which he has been winning for his exotic breeds over the years. Such prizes can be a trophy such as a cup, a certificate or an implement used in livestock husbandry such as a gelder.

However, whereas the Agricultural and Trade Fair asserts Tau's superiority over some cattle farmers and his status as an elite local entrepreneur, his show animals are not bred on his farm; they have come from the Transvaal, where he bought them as his breeding stock. The Ministry of Agriculture does not see anything wrong with this practice. In common with general practice throughout Botswana, and possibly beyond, Tau drives four or five show animals from his farm, twenty miles to his home village, months before the fair. At his village he feeds them special cattle feed, which makes them gain condition within a short time. On the show day, the cattle look very attractive, well-kept and quite different from their condition when they came to the village from the farm. The impression that unwary observers make, which actually is the impression Tau wants them to have, is that he keeps high quality exotic breeds under very high management levels.

The economic purpose of Tau's participation in the Fair, namely, that he is advertising his exotic breeds, becomes clearer after the show. Once the fair is over, he tries hard to market his show cattle while they are still in their prime show condition. Occasionally, one or two people will buy a bull from him during the fair or immediately thereafter, while the atmosphere of excitement surrounding his fetching of the first prize is still high. He considers it a great loss to have to trek the animals back to the farm after spending so much money feeding them for the show. In 1985 and 1986, however, he was disappointed and drove at least half of his show bulls back to the farms after failing to find buyers during and after the show.

In the presentation of the settler cases, the problem that cordon fences pose for cattle producers was portrayed. The problem is not only limited to hampering cattle production and marketing. Tau complains that the fences inhibit him from participating in the national show, outside his home district, thus denying him the opportunity to break through his district elite trap into something approximating national elite status. 'Only the farmers in the south have the monopoly of showing their cattle at the national show. Consequently, we in the north are unknown as exotic breeders' he says. In a bid to project fully the deprivation that he suffers on account of cordon fences, he runs into the problem of making statements which are not altogether correct, such as the assertion that he is the best breeder in the Tuli Block. This is wishful thinking. Tau has never set foot on the farm of the Clarks to see what real breeding is like.

His inability to take part in the national show and his allegation that it is only the farmers in the south (where the national capital is) who have the privilege of showing their breeds, in the process gaining the advantage that such participation brings with it, is now examined. Even in the south there are some restrictions on cattle movement, although such restrictions are not as strict as they are in Tau's sub-district which is more prone to foot-and-mouth disease. But farmers in the south have the geographical advantage of proximity to the national capital. Due to poorly organised extension services throughout the country, proximity to the national capital is an advantage; information is received more quickly than for ranchers who are farther afield.

Although Tau's allegation that he is second to none as a producer of exotic breeds is clearly inconceivable, it leads, nevertheless, to a discussion of his manner of ranching. In spite of economic progress made in the livestock trade, he is still a very undercapitalised rancher, both in his own right and in relation to settler ranching. By highlighting the condition of Tau's farms, a background is provided against which his intention to produce exotic breeds must be seen. Such activity, as shown in previous chapters that dealt with settler ranching, demands a certain level of technology and management standards.

Tau's ranches, like those of most other local ranchers, are poorly kept in comparison with those of the settlers who are still farming in the Tuli Block. Locally owned ranches including both of Tau's are dilapidated. On both of his farms the perimeter fences are crumbling due to rotting poles which have not been replaced since he bought the farms. Adjacent farms have a common perimeter fence. Vorster, whose large farm shares a perimeter fence with both of Tau's farms and other farms belonging to different farmers, is constantly complaining that Tau and other local farmers fail to repair their sections of the jointly owned perimeter fences. But because Vorster has much to lose if his perimeter fences are not well kept, he finds himself repairing all of the fences that form the mutual boundary between his farm and those of his local neighbours.

Since he bought his farms, Tau has not constructed any new paddocks. For a rancher who is producing exotic breeds this failure to construct additional paddocks reveals a great deal. On his smaller ranch there is only one borehole and two camps to service 637 ha. of a ranch without a river frontage. His larger farm with its 3,000 ha. has two boreholes and three camps.

There is no information on the way his farms were used either by their settler owners before he bought them, or even by himself in the earlier period, when he used them largely for keeping the trade cattle, awaiting marketing to the abattoir. But in the mid-1980s when he was engaged in small-scale breeding, he used the ranches unconventionally. With a total of 3,637 ha. between them, the two farms had between seventy and ninety head of cattle, most of them cross breeds between exotic and indigenous species, with only a few pure breeds, mostly bulls. This small number of herds was not a drought aversion measure. It was unintentional. Tau had sold many of his stock to pay his increasing debts. He was also slaughtering some of them for his butchery in town. The small number of cattle was actually a sign of a crumbling economy. The recommended stocking rate on enclosed ranches is one livestock unit per 16 ha. But in 1986, Tau's stocking rate was one livestock per 52 ha.

Despite this low stocking rate, the range was not in prime condition. To avoid deterioration of the range, the cattle were grazed on both ranches in turn. The straight distance between the two farms is four miles, but because the cattle have to be trekked on the backline road to avoid traversing a portion of Vorster's farm which separates Tau's farms, the total walking distance is eight miles, an average of eight miles being considered a normal distance for cattle to walk in a day.

The standards of animal breeding on both Tau's farms are low in comparison with those on settler farms. In part, this is due to the low skills of his employees, whom he, without much knowledge of producing exotic breeds, has to supervise. The overseer who is an elderly man is a distant relative of Tau's and has responsibility for both farms. He lives with his wife in the ranch house on the smaller farm. At some unspecified time the refugee manager left the larger farm and on it lives a younger male employee who hails from Tau's sub-district. This employee lives in a self-provided hut, with his wife and three younger children. He is not a relative of Tau's and he assists the elderly man, the overseer. Both have no formal education but they are reasonably literate.

Their wages have not been disclosed but the younger herder complains that his are very low and are paid irregularly, sometimes once in three months, and even then, often not all the expected money is paid. Both workers receive sufficient food, although it is only maize meal, for themselves and their families with whom they live on the farm. As on other locally-owned ranches, they are allowed free use of milk for their own consumption. The only strict condition is that they do not milk exotic cows, whose milk must be used solely by their calves in order for them to grow fast. Tau's workers sell some of the excess milk, especially if they are able to turn it sour. It is sold to visitors and passers by. Tau does not seem to like the idea of his workers selling his cows' milk but because he accepts that they have to augment their meagre wages, he does not forbid them. Neither of the two workers has any cattle of his own. It is evident that they are both from poor backgrounds.

The daily chores of the two employees, who are virtually herders, are to tend the cattle, making sure that none are lost. They water them daily, and detick them irregularly as ticks appear. On his farms, Tau gives no food supplement to his cattle except salt. He claims to be doing so, yet in reality he does not. He personally directs the rotation of grazing from one camp to another. Because he spends most of the time in his home village, he sometimes leaves instructions specifying the dates when cattle should move from one paddock to the next. The separation of cows from bulls for purposes of controlled breeding is poorly done, as there are not enough paddocks. Consequently, calves are born at various times of the year, unlike on the more conventionally-managed settler farms (cf. Clark's profile). Because only the exotic bulls are kept on Tau's farms, whether or not a calf is pure or hybrid depends on the cow. Otherwise with such a mix of animals he would not be able to tell which calves were pure and which were not.

His cattle regularly receive medicine. On the farm, there is always a sizeable quantity of different types of vaccines and medicines. Whenever they are given, Tau, who visits his farms almost every weekend, oversees the innoculations. He rarely sleeps at his farms, perhaps because of his entrepreneurial duties in the village or maybe because of the condition of the ageing and badly-kept farm house. It has no lawn or vegetable garden, both of which are taken for granted in the homesteads of the settler ranches.

The fact that Tau's business may be regarded as a failed expansion manifests itself in many ways. First, neither of the mortgages of the two farms has been fully settled. In 1983, the National Development Bank, which funded the purchase of his farms, took a decision in the wake of a major drought, to give a moratorium to its debtors until the climate improved (see Thothe, 1985: 9). The interest, however, was not waived. On the other hand the commercial bank which lent him P10,000 to purchase breeding stock is insisting that Tau repay their loan because he had the opportunity to market his breeds during periods when restrictions on cattle movement were lifted. In 1989, it was being strongly rumoured that the same bank was about to institute legal proceedings against him. Tau himself also gave that impression in his comparison of the terms of the National Development Bank and those of the commercial bank which lent him the money.

He has tried unsuccessfully to sell his smaller farm. An attempt to sell the farm, for an entrepreneur such as Tau, is clearly a telling sign of economic decline. The manner in which he is selling the farm conveys the impression that he is concerned to protect his public image. Clandestinely, he is busy contacting likely buyers but he is failing, it is said, because his asking price is high. Second, in 1989, he was negotiating the sale of two of his retail establishments, the village restaurant and the town butchery.

Molema – the 'big man' of the village

Molema, a lesser traditional elite who made his fortune from migration, was not an entrepreneur but a cattle-rich petty traditional elite at the time of his entry into the Tuli Block. He was already being regarded as a 'big man' by the villagers and he cherished the idea greatly. Increasing his cattle numbers and improving the breed is what he clearly perceives as a firm basis for enhancing the 'big man' image. There is a basic difference between a 'big man' and an entrepreneur. As a 'big man', Molema does not, for instance, follow people or customers as does Tau, an entrepreneur.

But upon closer examination it appears that Molema is nothing more than a district elite who, in economic terms, is worth less than Tau. His failure to expand, stems in part from the constraints of his portfolio as a district elite without outside connections. This closely circumscribed portfolio means he is not a party to valued information. As a result, he is at risk when the state imposes restrictions on passage of livestock across the district. Lack of such vital information undermines the efforts of the district elite to plan more systematically for cyclical upheavals in the physical environment and disease outbreak, which, though more or less constantly expected, catch many farmers unprepared.

Second, Molema's profile highlights the difficulties faced by local ranchers who have no alternative sources of income when ranching goes through a cycle of economic difficulty. Beyond that, this profile unveils the unanticipated high cost of moving from the communal areas where cattle are produced more cheaply under the traditional system, to a fenced ranch where the cost of cattle production is comparatively high. Such a comparison of costs of production between the two land systems was not covered in Tau's case material. Alongside the revelation of the high cost of transforming from communal to freehold cattle farming is highlighted a related phenomenon, the complexity of assessing the viability of the ranches of opportunistic farmers, that is, those who, in search of available grazing, graze the same herd or part of it on both farms and cattleposts, at different times of year.

Molema is in his early fifties. After matriculating from high school in 1958, he worked outside Botswana as a clerk, returning home in 1972. With savings from his earnings he started a cattlepost in his home district near northern Tuli Block. His cattle soon multiplied and the suspicion grew that he had brought with him a lot of money, giving him the image of a rich man. Despite his matriculation, a high academic qualification in Botswana at that time, Molema did not take up any paid job in Botswana after he returned from outside the country. Rather, he concentrated on cattle production. This may have contributed to his 'big man' image.

As his cattle multiplied, he was short of grazing, especially after the effects of the drought were being felt from 1981 onwards. In 1981, he bought a 2,000-ha. ranch. The ranch has a store which Molema has not operated since he bought the farm.

The farm cost him P90,000 or P42 per hectare. Molema was given a National Development Bank loan to purchase the farm. The interest rate was set at 15 per cent per annum on the reducing balance. His own equity was P18,000, representing 20 per cent of the value of the farm. The annual premium was calculated to P15,000. However, after paying the equity upon buying the farm in 1981, Molema has never been able to pay any of his annual premiums. Consequently, by 1986 he owed the bank a total of P155,000 inclusive of interest and penalties for defaulting on premiums. Nor has he been able to make any of the improvements which his farm needs so desperately, such as three borehole engines. In 1986, his workers had to carry one engine from one borehole to another through all the four boreholes on his farm as the cattle were being rotated through the camps. Molema's large settler-built house needs not only renovations, as do most other settler-built houses on the now locally owned Tuli Block farms; it needs water reticulation as well.

The reason Molema gives for his inability to pay the premiums and to effect these desperately needed improvements on his farm, is that his farm is overstocked, so that the entire farming business is vulnerable. This, he says, is largely through no fault of his own. He states that he bought the farm in order to get grazing for his cattle in the face of the drought of the 1980s. But the way he stocked it shows both the pressure he was under, to remove his cattle from the hard hit communal areas, and the probability that he did not foresee the problems that cordon fences might pose to cattle movement. His home district is one of the most densely populated in the Central District, in terms of cattle stocking rates. It is also one of the most susceptible areas to drought. Inspired by his awareness of these facts, he put all his cattle (more than 400 head) into the farm as soon as he had bought it and then was restricted from moving them because foot-and-mouth disease broke out in that part of the country and cattle movement outside the Tuli Block was restricted. Ironically the movement in the reverse direction, from the communal areas into the Tuli Block was allowed.

In 1982, the restriction was briefly removed, but by then, Molema's cattle which had increased to more than 500 heads, had overgrazed the 2,000 ha. and had lost condition. Molema was left in a dilemma. There was a pressing need to relieve overstocking on his farm, yet he could not sell any of his animals because they were too lean. His cattlepost in the eastern sandveld had not a blade of grass; therefore he could not transfer cattle from the overstocked and overgrazed farm into it. To crown everything, the P15,000 premium was due and if he failed to pay it, he faced a penalty fee for defaulting. He was still determined not to sell any of his cattle, because those who did, virtually gave their beasts away for nothing. (Molema recalls how he saw such farmers sell their beasts for P40 a piece whereas the price in the countryside was normally P150 per beast at the time.)

The way Molema extricated himself from this dilemma shows how district elites manipulate the state administrative machinery at the district level for their personal benefit. It also illustrates the force of kinship in the alleviation of disaster among indigenous farmers. Molema, who is a brother of the chief of his sub-district, exploited that relationship and made a crucial step that saved him from impending bankruptcy. With his brother's influence he became a member of the Land Board, a state body that deals with the allocation of tribal land, and also allocates borehole sites to farmers for grazing purposes. Membership of his Land Board is a key position, as it is the Land Board of the country's largest District (see Figure 1.6) and has the largest share of the enviable western sandveld, the area on which the largest cattle expansion in the country has taken place.

Once on the Land Board, Molema, in line with the normal practice of elites, used his position to acquire a grazing site in the western sandveld where there was abundant grass but no surface water. He borrowed money – it is not clear from whom – and drilled a borehole which he also equipped. In 1984, he obtained permission and moved most of his cattle by truck to his borehole, in the western sandveld. He had already lost ninety of them inside the farm from drought; and had been unable to afford stockfeed.

In the western sandveld, farmers raise very large herds over a very short period of time, as indicated at the beginning of this chapter. However, Molema, who has already raised quite a number of cattle in his new cattlepost and is even contemplating sinking a second borehole at a different site in the sandveld, doubts very much whether he will ever be able to repay the National Development Bank loan. This overwhelming debt which now amounts to P155,000 has brought about an apparent change in his tactics, though a change he may have thought of some time ago. Expecting the farm will eventually be repossessed, he now hesitates to make any payments towards the loan. His tactic, consequently, is to keep as many cattle as possible out of the ranch so that if the ranch is repossessed, he will still keep most of his cattle.

In a sense, this tactic originates from the old Tswana custom of hiding part of the herd from public knowledge, thereby veiling the real magnitude of a farmer's wealth. Molema's view, which he expresses frankly, is that it is better for him to keep his cattle, the source of his livelihood, than to risk destitution by selling them in a bid to repay a loan which may still have a large outstanding balance after all the cattle are sold. In other words, given the option of choosing between the ranch and the cattle, he would choose the cattle. Molema's fate now hangs in the balance and it may be that until he has either raised many more cattle in the sandveld or, on the other hand, failed to do so, that he will be able to decide what action to take concerning the farm loan. By then, of course, the farm may have been repossessed.

Like most self-image makers, such as Tau, Molema has a social side on which he tries to assert his pre-eminence over his peers or those who have the same source of livelihood as he. And, as turns out with many such local ranchers, such self-assertion becomes too costly. For example, despite his financial predicament, Molema travelled 200 miles, in 1986, to buy a pure brahman bull on a farm in Kimberley, South Africa. Responding to the question why he did not buy one from the established Tuli Block breeders such as Charles, he justified his action by alleging that Tuli Block settler breeders are often dishonest and, according to him, discriminate against locals. He explained further that such settlers produce both pure and hybrid bulls, which are penned in different kraals for sale purposes. When a local buyer comes, he is taken by the settler to the kraal with hybrids and told that he is being sold pure breeds at a discount price. On the contrary, says Molema, European customers are always sold pure breeds or whatever they ask for.

The manner in which Molema uses his farm contradicts the 'big man' image that he is building in the village. His use of the farm reflects an undercapitalised farmer who is unable to make the best of the ranch. The undercapitalisation manifests itself in his arable production, in the condition of the farm property and in the type of labour that he uses.

Unlike his settler neighbour, Vorster, and his local neighbour, Pitso, Molema has not been planting crops on his farm though it was extensively used for arable production by its previous Afrikaner owner. Again the reason is that he is undercapitalised. In the 1985–6 planting season, for the first time he tried to produce sorghum on his farm. That year had had sufficient rains to grow quickly maturing crops such as beans and groundnuts. However, both these crops need either more labour or expensive machinery, neither of which options Molema could afford. He therefore chose to plant a species of sorghum which requires a smaller workforce but one which took longer to ripen. More seriously, Molema, like Tau, did not even own a tractor or any farming implements. He was forced to wait for Pitso who has a tractor, to finish ploughing and planting before he could hire his tractor. For that reason, Molema ploughed too late when the moisture, which had been less than average, was even further reduced. Consequently, his attempt to produce the crop was unsuccessful; on 10 ha. (25 acres) he got only twelve bags of 70 kg each.

The kind of labour that Molema used for harvesting his crop shows that his economic expansion is based within his family. To harvest the crop he was helped by his elder sister and two nieces. When they had finished threshing (manually) they filled grain into bags by hand. The agreement was that they would not be paid money, but would be given a certain number of bags of crop each, depending on the size of the harvest. As stated above, the total was only twelve bags.

Typical of local ranchers in the Tuli Block, Molema relies very heavily on his kinship network for freehold farm labour (see Tau's profile above and Pitso's later). Although his two herders come from the same village ward as himself, they are not his relatives but his subjects. (The concept of a subject is explained later in the analysis.) The overseer of these two herders, however, is a distant cousin of Molema's. All three of them, the two unmarried young men of around twenty-five to thirty years of age and Molema's cousin who is married with two little children, live in the workers' quarters. Because Molema's farm is not as big as that of Vorster or of the Clarks, there are no quarters for herders other than the one near the rancher's homestead.

Interestingly, Molema's elder sister and his two nieces who helped him with the arable crop did not live in the workers' quarters but in the rancher's house. This suggests that he regarded them not as his workers but as part of his nuclear family. This conjecture seems to be confirmed by their payment arrangements, their reward being dependent on the size of the harvest and thus differing structurally from the set wages of the herders, who are hirelings. In addition, they enjoyed the privileges of the farm owner such as eating the oranges from the orchard.

Molema the 'big man', does not pay his herders higher wages than does a 'small man'. The exception is apparently his distant cousin who had to be induced to come and live on the ranch. (The actual wages were not disclosed.) Nevertheless, the herders complained that they were underpaid, and besides being low, the wages were paid irregularly. It may be thought that Molema's failure to pay wages regularly stems from the fact that he does not have a regular income. Such consideration falls apart once one recalls that even Tau, who as a multiple entrepreneur has a regular cash flow, fails to pay his farm workers regularly. One is tempted to note a general trend among local farmers of paying their herders irregularly.

The turnover of Molema's herders is low, notwithstanding his irregular payment. All three herders that were in his service in 1986 had joined him earlier in the communal areas, where they looked after his cattle. They were merely transferred to the ranch on the same wages they had been receiving in the cattlepost. They came into the ranch with their cattlepost privileges which include, especially, free maize flour, sufficient to feed them and their dependants who constantly visit them, and free use of as much cow milk as is available after Molema has fetched the amount of it that he needs for his own family in the village. Unlike Vorster, the large multiple entrepreneur, Molema, with a much smaller ranching venture is not concerned with what his workers do in their spare time or who they choose to bring into their living quarters.

Overall, the standard of ranching on Molema's farm, in particular animal husbandry, is low. One reason is that, like Tau who also maintains low ranching standards, Molema is an absentee farmer. Since 1982 when he became a member of the Land Board, he has been busy with its affairs, which have carried him all over the district. However, even before he became a Land Board member, he did not live on his farm. In the following chapter, the relationship between undercapitalisation and absenteeism of local ranchers is argued although these are other factors involved in absenteeism. The point made in this profile is that in spite of the overall consideration of the local freehold farmers, to develop not just the farm but their entire economy, the level of management on their farms, as reflected in Molema's, has suffered as a result of their absenteeism.

Deticking for instance, is done only when cattle are visibly infested with ticks. Unlike settler ranches, where the owners are either resident on the farm or are able to employ an experienced farm manager (e.g. Benson), on Molema's farm, and on Tau's, the normally routinised farm activities such as deticking, feeding animals with cattle feed and vaccinating calves at birth are performed irregularly. In particular, animal food supplement is crucial on Molema's farm in view of the shortage of grass discussed earlier.

Molema seems to have achieved some success in his bid to gain recognition as the 'big man' of the village. His greatest success was in 1986, when he was asked by cattle producers in his home village to talk to the Minister of Agriculture, asking him to give more lenient loan repayment terms for farmers, in view of the current major drought. The minister sympathised with Molema and took up the matter with his cabinet colleagues. This positive response by the government boosted respect for Molema and his social image. An outcome of his meeting with the minister was the scrapping of certain minor loans which farmers received during the drought and a longer moratorium from the National Development Bank on farm purchase loans.

Kgari – the traditional elite-cum-entrepreneur

Kgari's case is the profile of an educated traditional notable, whose socio-economic status as well as ambition for power and prestige, are much higher than those of either Tau or Molema, the lesser district elites. This is the profile of a man who has tried unsuccessfully to transform from the position of district elite, into the position, not of national elite, but that of international elite. Although in effect a district elite, Kgari already considers himself a national elite.

The discrepancy between the way people view him and the way he views himself highlights a problem that has been brought about by the change from traditional rule of the chiefs before independence to democratic rule in a new state after independence. Before independence, chiefs were the centre of authority, power and wealth within the entire society in their territories. After independence, they lost their social status as a result of the emergence of new elites in a changed social setting. Not all chiefs have accepted their reduced social status. Of course, most of them still wield social influence and, for that reason, some of them mediate as if they still held political authority. In other words chiefs still consider themselves as part of the state and hence as national rather than district elites.

Chiefs are indeed quite right to regard themselves as part of the state. The government considers them to be an important and integral part of the state linking it with the people. Nevertheless, the democratic arrangement of the post-colonial state has transferred to elected local government bodies most of the functions formerly perfomed by chiefs. The effect has been to reduce the power and status of chiefs. In practice, they have moved down the social ladder from a position of national elite to that of district elite. One prominent chief of a major tribe chose to resign his position as chief and become a politician, once it dawned on him that he had become merely a figure-head in his territory, and no longer the powerful traditional ruler that he had been for many years under colonial rule.

In spite of political changes, traditional rulers still command respect, especially within their own tribes. Naturally, they are keen to retain such respect as long as they can. Within this context, Kgari, as a traditional elite, wishes to maintain the social hierarchy. Because of this, his reasons for buying a freehold farm may be different from that of most other local ranchers, even though they too crave the kind of prestige he is after. While they are out to climb the social ladder, he is out to defend a social position which he has earlier held.

Kgari's traditional status, education, and close familial tie with a key figure in the government, all give him respect and credibility when seeking credit facilities. Because he is an entrepreneur as well as a notable, he has made connections with both local and foreign personalities. And, whereas most failed local ranchers are victims of drought and its related state policy, his total failure to expand, together with his subsequent bankruptcy are largely a result of his over-reaching himself in an effort to assert his superiority not over other district elites such as himself, but over the national elites with whom he is in competition.

At the end, Kgari's close relation, who used to be highly placed in government, is no longer in office, and Kgari goes bankrupt because he lacks the protection which would assure him a continuation of state backing for success as an entrepreneur. One problem, characteristic of most state-backed entrepreneurs, and one that has already been highlighted in the comparison between the alternative settler entrepreneurs, is that he does not establish a self-sustaining enterprise. Enterprises of national elites are continuously protected against entrepreneurial hazards as long as their owners remain tied to the state. For an important reason, I did not observe Kgari in the Tuli Block, and, consequently, I do not give any detailed account of his ranching practices, beyond noting the developments he made on his farm in an effort to produce exotic breeds.

Kgari is the son of a once famous and powerful traditional notable. He holds a university degree from a prestigious British university. For about fifteen years his very close kin held a position of high authority in the nation as a state elite. In that time, fortune seemed to favour Kgari and he was engaged in a number of economically important projects which made him money and gave him the appearance of a successful entrepreneur. He left his post in the tribal administration which he had been holding for his elder brother, and went to re-organise and manage his late father's estates, hoping to bring back the family's fame and dignity. With his inspiration, a family ranching company was formed along the lines of the Clarks' family firm. Provision was made for the post of a salaried manager who was to be a family member. The first such manager was Kgari's younger brother, but Kgari, who had himself joined the civil service, soon resigned and took over from his younger brother.

As manager of his family company, Kgari's first task was to sell most of the family's numerous head of cattle in the communal areas and with the money buy two freehold farms for the company, in the northern part of the country. He and his family were among the very first locals to buy a freehold farm. His close kin in government had bought a farm in the Tuli Block a year earlier. The family company did well, specialising in beef animals which were sold to the abattoir. During this time Kgari, a highly venerated social figure both within the former chiefdom and beyond, was appointed to membership of many committees of public bodies. These included the BMC Board and the Board of a foreign commercial bank. He had also invested privately in other business ventures as a shareholder in a large company, and also as a partner in a cattle agency which had its main office in the abattoir's town. (At the time, the country's abattoir had no branches; it now has two, one in the northern part of the country, and the other in north-western Botswana).

In the mid-1970s, the members of Kgari's family decided to dissolve their company and sub-divide its assets among themselves. Following this, and apparently in a bid to assert himself as more than a district elite with a social life tied and limited to the former chiefdom, Kgari bought his own farm, measuring 4,000 ha. in the Tuli Block. He obtained a National Development Bank loan to pay for the farm. It is not clear what type of cattle he initially kept on the farm but after some time he stocked it with grazier scheme cattle.

These last were cattle that the state entrusted to farmers of means, the idea being that the farmers would keep the offspring of the animals and also retain, at the time of marketing the cattle, whatever excess there then was in the value of the cattle, and their value when they were entrusted to the farmer. The programme had been initiated as a contingency measure to help the livestock industry. By participating in the scheme, farmers would recover from the drought. The abattoir, and therefore the state, would benefit from selling to its markets better quality meat than would have been the case if there had been no such programme.

Later, while still owning the Tuli Block farm, Kgari moved into meat retailing. He bought a butchery in a town about fifty miles from his farm and settled in a large modern house which he had bought in that town. As already stated, in times of drought, some settler entrepreneurs sold through their butcheries meat from cattle that came from their farms. Indeed, one of the largest settler entrepreneurs in the country prefers to sell meat from his cattle through his butchery rather than market the cattle to the abattoir. The settler entrepreneur in question makes more money in this way. It is not clear if there was any such structural connection between the farm and the butchery in Kgari's case.

The advantage of education that Kgari had over most other local ranchers showed itself best in the manner in which he practised ranching. Unlike most local ranchers who have failed to develop their farms, Kgari, perhaps with social hierarchy in mind, set about developing his farm with the aim of making it a model of a conventional breeding ranch producing expensive and prestigious exotic animals. His contention is that most local ranchers are influenced in their management by a cattlepost mentality. In order to counter local management standards and uphold conventional standards of a cattle breeding farm, especially one that produces exotic breeds, he recruited a European manager from South Africa and increased the farm's grazing units from the three camps, that he had found on it, to ten paddocks.

As shown in the profile of the Clarks, constructing paddocks is an expensive undertaking. Before long, Kgari bought exotic breeds from South Africa, another very expensive move. Almost simultaneously he invested heavily in a costly joint venture, but one which would both elevate his social image and, if successful, turn him into a large international entrepreneur. A substantial amount of the over one million pula capital was provided by his partner, an entrepreneur from outside Botswana. As Kgari himself explained to the media, he put almost everything he had into the project which had been envisaged and planned for over five years. In the midst of all this he took the occasional working holiday abroad with his family.

Once he had made his last and heaviest investment in the joint venture, his debts were enormous. His highly placed kin in the government had left office a few years before Kgari launched the joint multi-million pula venture. After his kin had left, Kgari's entrepreneurial career took a nose-dive. His problems, most of which surfaced simultaneously, had a chain reaction effect and in no time he was insolvent. Unfortunately, he was one of the elite who had lost some of the grazier scheme cattle that had been entrusted to him.

The BMC took legal action against such farmers including him. To raise money to settle the debt, he sold his shares in the private company he had invested in. He had already lost his Tuli Block farm to the National Development Bank, who repossessed it once he had failed to pay the premiums during a rainy period before the drought of the mid-1980s. The southern part of the Tuli Block had experienced some rainfall in the late 1970s while the northern part, where the other district elites in this study have their farms, had not. As such, the National Development Bank does not seem to have been acting arbitrarily or in a way that would suggest prejudice against Kgari when it repossessed his farm but not those of the other two district elites.   '

Under further financial pressure, Kgari sold his butchery and his large house in the town where he had lately been residing. It seems today as if the nation has accepted Kgari's economic failure. In the aftermath of his success, he has not been given any public appointment such as a membership of a public committee, a show of respect he had enjoyed before.

Kgari's failure to repay the farm's mortgage while he had the opportunity to do so before the drought, suggests something important about his perception of the way the state deals with elites. It would appear, from his actions, that he had expected some favour, such as the writing-off of loans as bad debts. He may, in fact, have seen the state do just that for certain elites. He may, therefore, have been hoping that all elites would receive the same treatment from the state. In the analysis of the state and elites, it has been shown how hard it is for the district elites to manipulate the state in the way their more highly-placed colleagues, the national elite, can do.

Having failed in this enterprise, Kgari is now turning to arable farming in the communal areas where his family has large tracts of arable fields.

ANALYSIS OF DISTRICT ELITES

It is necessary to analyse at this stage the peculiar features of the district elites as they have appeared in the profiles, because some of these character-istics do not emerge in the profiles of those entrepreneurs that are still to be presented, namely the national elite and the non-elite. The analysis takes the form of a comparison and a contrast of the three district elites. To enhance the comparative analysis, some issues from the profiles of the alternative settler entrepreneurs, as and when the need arises, will be brought into the discussion. Emphasis is placed on further explication of the term *elite* in its broader scope and practical sense. The aim is to demonstrate the respects in which these entrepreneurs are elites, and, in the process, the mechanisms of rising into the position of elite and maintaining that position, are discussed.

The analysis here does not follow the order in which the cases were presented. This time, traditional elites are discussed first, next the upwardly mobile entrepreneur, and third, the village 'big man'. Finally all three are compared.

The traditional (chiefly) elite as an entrepreneur

The term 'elite' is more easily visualised in the context of 'traditional elites' because of their unquestionable chiefly status, a social superiority that is taken for granted. Traditional elites are what they are not through achievement or success as are the newly-emerged elites, but by virtue of their status of birth. In Botswana, where chiefdoms were once powerful, autonomous en-tities or 'nation states' within a British-ruled Protectorate (see Tlou, 1974: 21), such chiefly elites had their exclusive position which earned them income within the hierarchy of the administration of the chiefdom.

As chiefs, or his closest relatives, they were allocated responsibility for the performance of which they received rewards in the form of tributes whose size depended, partly, on the resources of the chiefdom. They were the core of the traditional establishment and did not usually take up paid employment outside the chiefdom's administration, jobs outside the adminis-tration of the chiefdom being rated socially inferior to their traditional and venerated positions which also afforded them a relatively high standard of living.

Kgari's profile indicates that despite a traditional elite's university qualifications, the alternative to his traditional position in post-colonial Botswana is either a dignified enterprise as shown in his family company and his investments in public companies, or else a high political position that he is now seeking within the central government. His brief stay in the civil service where he held a post that was below that of national elite suggests that he did not regard the job as appropriate for him. Besides material gain for a chiefly elite in the traditional establishment, there was the very important issue of social rank in one's chiefdom. Although some commoners could raise more cattle than the chiefly elite (see Parson, 1979: 34) authority of command, which was asserted through possessing more wealth than one's subjects, had to remain with the chiefly elite, as did other chiefly elite advantages.

An example of benefits for chiefs was that they were the first beneficiaries of the state-initiated bull subsidy scheme, a livestock development programme, making them the first owners of improved cattle. Again, both in Kgatleng and the Central District, the chiefly elite were the first to take advantage of state-provided boreholes which had been sunk originally as a drought relief measure in the less densely populated western sandveld (see Peters, 1983: 15 for the Kgatleng case and Hitchcock, 1982: 9 for the Central District case).

Kgari, who typifies high-ranking chiefly elites, goes into entrepreneurship and into ranching having benefited from the foregoing state initiatives. But it is typical of a member of the chiefly elite that he brings into entrepreneurship an appetite for the highest social rank and privilege. His appetite for social rank was whetted still further by his education. In line with the common policy of the time whereby children of the chiefly elite were given the best education outside the country, Kgari was sent to a prestigious British university where his kin who was also a state elite had studied earlier. While in Britain, Kgari had been exposed to the lifestyle of the English aristocracy. Both of these experiences, education and exposure to a loftier lifestyle, have become a part of his own experience and seem to have enlarged his understanding of a chiefly elite. Kgari's attempt to live up to the ideal standard of a sophisticated traditional elite, one that is different from most others, pushes him into what may be seen as excessive ambition.

The problem of elites trying to climb higher is not by any means confined either to the chiefly elite or to the other two district elites in this study, both of whom are also its victims. In Seychelles, middle-class entrepreneurs attempted to emulate the upper-class and actually cut links with the lower class among whom they had friends and kin (Benedict and Benedict, 1982: 177). But they did not escape the fate that befell the chiefly elite, because emulating people in an income group higher than their own resulted in them living beyond their means. Their problem, which is also Kgari's, is that they ignored the all-important fact that expenditure, including a flamboyant life-style, has to be financed out of the spender's income and this last must always exceed such expenditure.

After observing self-aggrandisement among members of Jehovah's witnesses in Zambia at the expense of the expansion of their business, Long cautions that higher living standards or education should never be confused with wealth (Long, 1968: 18). Cohen makes the same point: form is not to be confused with substance. He argues that the fact that different societies and communities within the society may manifest apparently similar forms does not suggest that they have become culturally homogeneous (Cohen, 1985: 37). Even though wealth, education and high living standards can go together in some cases, they are still mutually exclusive. To be the elite that Kgari wanted to be, he needed all three. Having only education and a traditional status that was no longer financially backed, he lived a high standard of living at the expense of wealth.

In order to uncover more fully the ambitions as well as explain the goals of a high-ranking traditional elite, a comparison of the traditional with the national elite is presented. The purpose is to bring into the analysis a crucial phenomenon, namely, competition, both within the category of district elites and between the two categories of district and national elite. The broader spectrum of national elite is reserved for the next chapter.

As already observed, one distinction between a district and a national elite is that a district elite has influence that is limited to local government, while a national elite is a part of the national government and therefore has influence at a national level. Because national elites operate from within the national government machinery in their capacity as heads of parastatal bodies, senior civil servants and politicians, they are able to influence and formulate national policy in their favour. For instance, they could broaden the scope of state and parastatal financial institutions such as the National Development Bank and the Financial Assistance Policy to include enterprises in which they want to invest.

To cite an example, grazier scheme cattle, originally meant for ranch owners, eventually went to cattleposts through pressure from national elites who did not have ranches. This bears testimony to the influence of national elites over wider areas within the country in comparison with that of their district colleagues. Their influence extends into rural areas as well. As Werbner points out, national elites have gone to great lengths to extend the organic link between themselves and the countryside (Werbner, 1988: 4).

Whereas district elites do the same at local government level, and whereas there are many advantages that a district elite might derive from the local government to expand his cattle industry as Molema's profile has indicated, the major shortcomings of the district elite arise from the narrowness and limited nature of the services and state programmes that a local government machinery handles in comparison with that of the national government. Thus, a clearer distinction between the two types of elite emerges when one considers the implications of being one kind of elite or the other, that is, a national or a district elite.

Due to the autonomy of the chiefdoms in the colonial era, a traditional elite had a status which is equivalent to that of a national elite in the post-colonial era. Even though Werbner is correct in his assertion that the end of the Protectorate did not bring about an end to the tribe (Werbner, 1988: 4), in social terms things have, for the traditional elites, changed for the worse. A problem for this kind of elite is that of adjustment to the major political transformation which not only eroded their influence but also their social support as indicated below.

Kgari's difficulty in accepting what is now a watered-down form of elitism is aggravated by his education and experience in Britain, both of which had prepared him for a place, not in the local government structure, but as a national elite in something equivalent to central government. Consequently, there is an incongruency between the actual social position of Kgari and the position that he envisages for himself. His goals remain those of a national elite, yet the harsh reality is that society treats him as a district elite.

The difficulty of the superior traditional elite in adjusting to political transformations, which left them with lowered social status and a position that had also lost its mysticism in post-colonial Botswana, has been a widespread feature in the country. One example was cited in Kgari's profile. McCartney relates another in which the chief of a major chiefdom in southern Botswana insisted that he should still be responsible for allocating land as his predecessors had always done before him. The chief was speaking immediately after a senior civil servant accompanying him had finished reading to the audience the new Land Act of 1978 which transferred the powers of allocating land from chiefs to democratically elected Land Boards (McCartney, 1978).

As Picard also states, traditional elites and other cattle barons regarded themselves as heirs to the post-colonial government (see Picard, 1980: 316–30). As if echoing Picard's claim, Kgari's own new chief, given the throne during the post-colonial era, has not made himself available for the traditional position, preferring instead to remain in his profession which has given him the status of a national elite.

Under such circumstances, part of Kgari's problem can be seen as a failure to adjust to a changed political situation, from colonial to post-colonial. He typifies the superior aristocrats who have become the victims of political dynamics or social development. Kgari's problem is that despite all indications to the contrary, he lives the life of the national elite he thinks himself to be. He mediates in an assumed role. It would appear that because of the incongruency between his actual and envisaged status, he has over-reached himself and mediated in a way that has resulted in his liquidation.

In concluding the analysis of the traditional elite, the question of the purpose of buying the ranch is re-examined. Throughout the analysis the purpose for which the ranch was used, namely to enhance Kgari's status and image as an elite, rather than merely to produce animals is shown. Obviously, the way in which property is used does not in any way imply that to be the only purpose for which it was intended. Kgari, for instance, might have borrowed money from the bank in order to activate his other business, using the ranch as collateral security. The sudden and simultaneous collapse of all his enterprises, especially, suggests that his businesses were tied to one another in this way. As Kgari himself admits, there are other reasons for local ranchers owning a freehold farm. The real reason does not always lie on the surface. What the farm is used for, even though it may not be what was originally intended, becomes crucial to understanding the aim and goals as well as the limitations of the rancher.

Kgari's main problem was to mediate in a role that was loftier than his real one and he did this without sufficient capital to back his claim to the ranks of a new national elite in a social structure that had changed for the worse for him in the post-colonial state. His aims and goals became both idealist and utopian in the new society. Like most local ranchers, Kgari underestimated the cost of producing exotic breeds (something that more experienced settlers like Benson and Vorster were careful to note) and he ended up intentionally or unintentionally recruiting a European manager whose high wages he could ill afford.

The recruitment of the European manager introduced onto Kgari's farm a development which was dissimilar to the ranching styles of all local Tuli Block farmers; he cut ties with the communal areas. Unlike other locals, he did not keep a cattlepost. It would appear that he wanted to make a total transformation overnight from communal to freehold cattle farming. To someone who perceived his status as being that of a national elite, such a choice was natural but a great deal was needed to make the option work. Reviewing his mediation, it is apparent that he is a traditional elite whose education and traditional portfolio have not prepared him for business and, in particular, his education is not appropriate for farming. As van der Ploeg observes, farm labour is a conscious goal-oriented activity (van der Ploeg, 1990: 259).

The upwardly mobile entrepreneur

The upwardly mobile entrepreneur differs from the traditional elite in many significant ways. First of all, whereas the elitism of the superior aristocrat is taken for granted because it is based on the tradition and social structure of the tribe or the chiefdom, and is genealogically derived, the elitism of the upwardly mobile entrepreneur, typical of any new or emergent elite, is acquired on the basis of the success of the entrepreneur, and because it depends on personal success, it is more precarious and needs a better and closer management of social relationships than the more formal traditional elitism.

The two types of elite are nevertheless linked. Although Kgari and Tau do not appear to be engaged in any competition, there is nevertheless a connection between the decline of traditional elitism and the emergence of new elitism: both are the result of political dynamics linked with the movement from a confederation of autonomous 'nation states' (that Botswana used to be during the colonial era), to its present post-colonial structure of a unitary state with centralised authority. As stated before, Tau's rise from the social position of a commoner to that of an elite may be regarded as an aspect of social development that is based on this political dynamic.

To focus on the making of an upwardly mobile elite who begins from the level of a commoner, first the type of elite that Tau represents needs to be explained: he is a 'new elite', but then there are many kinds of 'new elite' as already indicated. From his profile, Tau is clearly an innovator because he evolved a way of breaking the monopoly of the settler cattle buyers in his home region by bridging the gap in the prices paid by the settlers on the one hand and the Botswana Meat Commission on the other. Defining such a social innovator among Jehovah witnesses in Zambia, Long writes:

> the social innovator is a person who manipulates other persons or resources, discovers new channels for exploitation or utilises 'traditional' relationships and values, in an attempt to achieve some new type of goal, or who devises some novel means to attain some already recognised end. (Long, 1968: 5)

A paraphrase of Long's quotation is that a social innovator discovers a new way of providing a social service and to do that he manipulates people. The traditional elite was at the centre of social service during his time, the colonial era. He controlled people. Thus, the operative characteristic of an elite is that he must control or manipulate the people in order to provide them a service. In his role as a cattle trader, Tau was providing a social service. He had successfully wooed customers from some settler traders who were providing the same service. As such, he was at the centre of a socio-economic network which also gave him a model position in the economic space.

A description of Tau as an elite may not be complete until the rank or size of his model position in his economic space is also explained. The rank of a traditional elite depends on his position in the family's genealogy and is reflected in the level and range of authority that he has over the tribe. In the same way, the rank of a new elite is determined by the level or order of goods and services that he handles on behalf of the society. In Tau's sub-district, cattle trading had the highest place in the hierarchy of socio-economic services and that automatically made Tau, who was dealing in cattle, a high-ranking new elite in his area of operation.

A crucial feature of cattle trading which gave it pre-eminence over minor trades such as restaurants and butcheries was its links outside the sub-district. As Barth aptly observes, the entrepreneurial activity may be under-stood as a response and adaptation to the unequal economic relationship of the local community with the outside (Barth, 1963: 15). This means that Tau, who now forms this link, becomes a 'channel of conversion' to borrow Barth's term. He is a broker, a middleman, and hence, a new elite.

The whole issue of the link between the local community and the outside world unveils yet another major phenomenon in our understanding of new elites, namely, the very process through which they emerge, or the way in which they are made. This takes the analysis back to the link between social development and the emergence of new elites. As already suggested, a link exists between the decline of the traditional elite and the emergence of the new. Once the traditional way of life gave way to a democratic one, social organisation was reconstituted differently, with emphasis on individual rather than communal production. This new social organisation in which the tradi-tional elite was no longer absolutely dominant, although still influential, brought about a new opportunity structure which enabled the innovative individual to rise to the position of a new elite through enterprise.

However, successful entrepreneurship also demands the ability to mesh internal and external factors (see Long, 1968: 14–18; Mahoney, 1977: 310). Tau succeeded in meshing these factors well. In his case, the external factors were the many cattle whose owners were seeking ways of marketing them following the drought of 1971–2. But as Mahoney rightly states, Tau's success cannot be explained solely by reference to drought (Mahoney, 1977: 315). There was also an internal factor, Tau's own innovative quality, which was as important as the external in making Tau an elite. Though not the only small general dealer before the 1971–2 drought, he was different from the others in that he was more innovative than they were. The fact that he ascended into a higher level of a cattle trader while they did not, suggests that he had something which they lacked.

While both Mahoney and I accept that the making of a new elite has to do with social mobility, I do not share Mahoney's view regarding the signific-ance of Tau's rise to the position of elite. Mahoney maintains that Tau was never a minor trader (see Mahoney, 1977: 323). In fact, Mahoney holds that minor and major traders in Tau's village were not 'rungs on a career ladder'. He insists that small traders remained small while large ones such as Tau went into business already as large traders. Mahoney then argues that for major traders, social mobility has to be explained in terms of their participation in an historically unique series of events rather than their passage through any fixed hierarchy of positions and uses this point of view to criticise Frankenberg. The latter suggests that Paine's two kinds of trader, the *freeholder* and *free enterpriser* (which resemble the minor and major traders), represent stages in a career from peasant to large-scale entrepreneur (see Frankenberg, 1967: 64).

The contention here based on field data analysis and a review of Mahoney's own data, is that Mahoney's argument does not make the point that he wants to make. Consequently, it does not in any way challenge Frankenberg's stand which I fully endorse. The fact is that both minor and major traders contemporaneously participated in what Mahoney calls 'the historically unique series of events'. The weakness of Mahoney's position is that he does not show what triggered the differentiation between the small and the large traders. The facts of his profile of Tau and this profile of the same elite concur that Tau started from the bottom. Both agree that Tau had to emigrate in search of paid employment before he could raise his starting capital and that Tau started in a small way as a restaurant owner, later rising to the higher entrepreneurial level of cattle trader. As Mahoney himself points out, Tau made wealth over a short period of time so that when the drought came he had made and accumulated more money than most other small entrepreneurs, hence, there was no competition for the cattle trade between him and his fellow village traders (Mahoney, 1977: 316). It would appear, therefore, that contrary to Mahoney's later assertion, Tau did move from the position of low rank entrepreneur to that of a high rank trader, very much along the lines of Frankenberg's model.

Mahoney makes yet another statement whose import, if it ever was correct, has been seriously undermined by the pattern of entrepreneurial activities in the 1980s. He ascribes the failure of some traders to their external partners (Mahoney, 1977: 312). His argument is that such traders failed because they shared profits with their external partners. Indications in the 1990s are that some of the most prosperous entrepreneurs in the country are those who are financially backed by external partners. Again, the history of early settlement in the Tuli Block shows that settlers who were financially backed by Johannesburg cattle buyers expanded their ranches much more than those who were not. Mahoney may be right but it is possible that he is unduly influenced in his argument by Barth's notion of bordermanship and entrepreneurship, namely, that an entrepreneur, by crossing sphere boundaries, may suffer repercussions (Barth, 1967). It appears that Mahoney accepts the mould of Barth's analysis, without critically analysing the circumstances of his case material.

The village 'big man'

The assertion that the emergence of the new elite is a result of the fading of the aristocrat, acknowledges that the aristocrat still wields influence within his chiefdom. Molema's profile takes this argument further by indicating that whereas, at the centre of the chiefdom, the superior aristocrat is becoming somewhat disillusioned with his waning influence, the situation is different at the periphery of the chiefdom where post-colonial social organisation still places the traditional elite at the centre of social life. This phenomenon has to do with the mechanism and pace of the development of the centralised post-colonial state and its equally centralised authority at the nation's seat of government, which spreads outwards to the remote areas where the authority of the state is less felt and the traditional authority more strongly felt.

Eventually, in its structure and operation, the mechanism for centralised authority creates what may be loosely termed the dualism of power, in which the periphery is controlled by traditional or district elites, while the central government is under the domination of state or national elites. This is not to deny that traditional elites are a part of the post-colonial government structure; it is merely to observe that their sphere of influence has been circumscribed to districts, away from the mainstream of central national development.

I go further and assert that the existence of separate development plans within the nation, the National Development Plan and the District Development Plan, even though they are meant to be mutual and complementary, would seem to be an admission by government, of this dualism of authority. Local government is still run by the state but in an indirect way, mainly through district elites who work in conjunction with traditional elites. The Land Board, for instance, is one of the most powerful organs of local government and is, as I have pointed out in the profile, dominated by traditional elites such as Molema. Contrary to the waning power of traditional authority at the central government level, Gulbrandsen states that it can be very powerful at the district level, especially over land issues (Gulbrandsen, 1984).

Molema is not as big a traditional elite as is Kgari. For him, there is clout in being counted among traditional elites. This is because as only a minor aristrocat who is not from the core of aristocracy, Molema has never fully enjoyed the full status of a traditional elite. In fact, he is seeking recognition not only as a wealthy man, but more importantly as a wealthy man of chiefly lineage. Aristocracy, minor though it may be, gives credence to his claim as a 'village big man' because then he is part of the expansion of political order. The grandeur of a traditional elite is receding faster at the nation's seat of government, but that does not worry Molema because in his village setting, aristocracy still means authority. It was on that basis that the community chose him to lead the delegation of farmers from his region to complain to the Minister of Agriculture about the payment of farm purchase loans during drought.

The community had many well-placed people to choose from; the local MP, or even Tau, an entrepreneur who commanded more material resources than Molema. There was also Molema's brother, the chief of the village. Although the whole idea might have been prompted by Molema himself, for their part, the people preferred him or co-operated with him because, as a chiefly figure, they regarded him as their natural and more permanent overseer.

The selection of Molema in the presence of his brother, the chief, is a point worth commenting upon. The chief certainly has more authority than Molema but the point is that he is not as large a cattle farmer as Molema. In the circumstances, Molema feels the pinch of the drought more than him. Even so, the chief might not have been too keen to go in person to see the minister. It might have served his purposes better for him to send his younger brother. This would also shield him from any repercussions by keeping him out of controversy. For such errands, the chief is safer using his kin who would then take the blame for any misadventure resulting fom the errand. It also makes the chief less controversial to his superiors, as they do not expect him to appear to exert too much pressure on the state to alter its established framework of alleviating drought. On the other hand, as long as his brother goes to meet the minister, the subjects in the territory are pleased with the chief.

What is happening here is that the two minor aristocrats are continuing to work together in complementary rules for their own good individually and as a family. In addition, by doing the errand on behalf of his brother, Molema is actually reciprocating his brother's assistance in making him a member of the Land Board, a move which saved him from the drought. Such mutual assistance among family members carries obligations. If one party fails to reciprocate, the familial bonds may break (Long, 1972: 18).

In comparison with the profiles of the two other district elites, the episode also illuminates a very important theoretical point with respect to the role of the family in the social change of the individual. It shows that a petty aristocrat need not break away from his family in order to 'develop'. In the case of the village 'big man', it is his family which actually helps him with the supervision of the farm. This kind of familism is certainly wanting in either the upwardly mobile entrepreneur who at best uses distant relatives as paid workers, or the superior aristocrat who has left his family behind in his quest for big business with international partners. Apparently, such a great aristocrat, once he passes through the stage of a family firm with a kinship ideology similar to the familist settler firm, goes on to the stage of individualism as characterised by the individualist settler firm.

But the contrast is even greater; the individualist settler firm still uses its professional family labour for which it pays wages at the going rate. The great aristocrat, given his lack of ranching knowledge and his desire to produce special animal breeds has to hire a professional worker. On the other hand, the 'village big man' starts in the usual way with the support of his kin, just as the superior aristocrat receives the support of his family in the early stages of his career. The 'village big man' is not yet big enough to break away from the kinship bond into an individualist stage. And just as it is not easy to say whether or not the familist settler firm will eventually break up into smaller individualist firms, so too, it remains to be seen whether a minor aristocrat must break away from his kinship network during an individualist stage.

One other major point has to be made about the elitism of the 'village big man'. His failure to participate in enterprise does not mean that he does not provide a community service. Just as an entrepreneur provides a service of one kind to the community, a minor aristocrat provides a service of another kind, intercession with the state on behalf of his people. In itself, such intercession is both a service and a means of controlling the people. Hence, the minor aristocrat is using his self-made wealth to reassert himself as an aristocrat in order to have a more natural reason to mediate on behalf of his tribal group.

An equally crucial point is why the 'village big man' is not involved in enterprise. A possibility is that he wants to avoid competition with Tau, a close kinsman. But a more likely reason is that enterprise is not Molema's priority, since he considers himself a different type of elite from Tau who has no aristocratic blood. As an aristocrat, Molema wants to achieve great things, just like Kgari, the superior aristocrat. He cannot afford to be involved in petty trade such as owning a small general dealer establishment, for example a restaurant. As a 'village big man' he wants to do 'big' things.

A point made in Barth (1963) about local entrepreneurs of northern Norway, and one that is valid in this study, is that a study of local entrepreneurs in a particular setting, is in effect a study of social change within the community. Also, the close association between entrepreneurs and the general leadership among Tuli Block local entrepreneurs is quite similar to what is observed within the Norwegian setting referred to above.

Having provided a brief analysis of some aspects of the district elites, and having highlighted further the concept of 'elite' and its frame, the profiles of two other entrepreneurs are presented, the executive-state elite and the non-elite. All major features of both profiles are analysed in depth in the following chapter. For that reason, there is not, unlike in the cases of the district elites above, any brief analysis following their presentation.

PULE – THE EXECUTIVE STATE-ELITE

In this profile the statist strategy of a prominent member of the executive state's national elite is exemplified. Pule is a former civil servant of the highest rank who became a leading politician and state policy maker. His strategy is statist in that it relies heavily upon the state for purposes of agricultural innovation and entrepreneurship. His entry into large-scale farming and his commercial breakthrough – both of which have been considerable, would otherwise not have been possible had he not first held a bureaucratic and later a high political office. It is the state to which this member of the national elite has turned for finance and privileged marketing.

All of this has been done publicly and astutely within the law, so far as can be assessed. His statist strategy is evident in his use of the state loan to obtain large financial grants to buy expensive modern farming machinery, to secure a protected and privileged market for his arable produce and to receive further state grants to pay his workers.

As a result, he operates his farm in a way which his less privileged fellow farmers, outside the state bureaucracy, cannot hope to emulate, even though some are more experienced farmers than him. Pule's advantage, which is the advantage of national elites in general, is information, not only on the available investment opportunities but also on the most effective ways of satisfying the conditions for qualifying for participation in such programmes. In this regard, his case is comparable with that of Charles, a settler national elite who was in partnership with the state. The cases of Pule and Charles contrast sharply with those of the district elites who are left at a disadvantage by their lack of information in a series of ways.

Whereas the district elites have failed to expand because, among other reasons, of lack of privilege, national elites typified by Pule succeed primarily because of privilege, and not so much because of efficiency. Pule's profile is unique in that while he keeps some cattle on his farm, his main focus is on arable production. He is being used by the state as a model farmer, a pioneer at the technological frontier of cash cropping.

Pule, married with one young daughter, hails from a village 15 miles from his farm. His father, an ordinary citizen without rank, lives in that village. Pule himself has a bottle-store and a cattlepost nearby. In the 1960s, he acquired a master's degree in economics from a British university and then joined the civil service. Ten years later, having risen to a senior and responsible position, Pule began, in stages, to buy a farm, now measuring 2,000 ha. The farm was bought from its previous owners, a South African land company.

In 1989, the legal transaction to buy the farm was completed, although by 1991 he had succeeded in paying only half of the farm's mortgage. The other half was still mortgaged to the National Development Bank, through whom the farm had been bought. Unlike the district elites who have generally failed to repay their ranch purchase loans, the national elite, exemplified by Pule, have either fully repaid these loans or are in the process of completing their payments.

After serving in a high position in the civil service to which he had been promoted a few years earlier, Pule retired sometime in the 1980s, in time to contest the national political elections at constituency level, as a candidate for the ruling party. By resigning from the civil service to become a politician in the ruling party, he was following the example of quite a few of his predecessors. He won in his constituency and thus changed from being a bureaucratic state elite to being a political state elite. In either position he remained a national elite. (In this study, the term state elite embraces the two portfolios of bureaucrat and politician, because in Botswana the holders of the two positions often share the same views, especially on patterns of social development. The close cooperation between bureaucrats and politicians as exemplified in part by the ease of movement from one position to another makes the two positions socially more or less equivalent.)

Once Pule had established himself in politics, he focused his farm activities on arable productivity, thus proving, contrary to convention, local farming in the Tuli Block is not completely monocultural, in that it does not only concentrate on livestock production. Under district elites, Molema, as was shown, has also made a frail start in producing crops on his farm. In due course, I show that another local farmer, Pitso, has more acreage under cultivation, although he, like the rest of the locals who cultivate crops in the Tuli Block, has not reached Pule's scale, sophistication and variety.

Already serving in his executive political portfolio, Pule sought and received a Financial Assistance Policy (FAP) grant for P100,000 which he used to construct a large grain storage house, to buy a tractor, a baling machine, a threshing machine and two water pumping engines. He purchased all the items from South Africa, where they are cheaper and more readily available. He was granted a further P50,000 to pay his workers for two years, as well as to service the machines. Pule was offered the grant under the category of a medium-scale project. This category did not require him to contribute any financial capital; his farm was regarded as enough capital qualification for him to be given the grant. So far, this has been the largest FAP grant to an individual in all of the Tuli Block. Following the departure from office of Kgari's kinsman who was superior, Pule is the only state elite of his standing in the Tuli Block.

This grant aroused a wave of strong criticism from other Tuli Block farmers and from the residents of the surrounding villages. Their criticism is that the state has favoured its own elite and discriminated against many other applicants in the Tuli Block and its surrounding villages who have requested FAP assistance but been denied it. In response to this criticism, Pule argues that he had been given the grant on the strength of the project proposal submitted to government by a firm of accountants which he employed. He insists that the grant had nothing to do with his status. Yet it remains possible that Pule, as an insider, did have advantageous knowledge and credibility. He would have been able to seek and obtain information, not only about the necessary, but also the sufficient conditions that must be met in order to qualify for the grant (see Douglas and Craig, 1983, for a fuller discourse on the power of information in entrepreneurship).

The problem of absenteeism dogs both district and national elites among local farmers. It also affects the productivity of their farms almost equally, except that in the case of national elites, access to more state financial assistance tends to veil the extent of the inefficiency of the entrepreneurs. With respect to Pule in particular, although also true for other local farmers in general, labour productivity is the one thing that is hardest hit by the elite's absenteeism. Because of the nature of his job, Pule has to live in the national capital, some 200 miles away from his farm. On his mixed farm more permanent staff are employed than on most locally-owned ranches where cattle raising is the sole farming activity. He has employed five permanent employees: the manager, crop foreman, tractor driver and two cattle herders. Pule avoids producing exotic breeds although he occasionally buys improved cattle from local and settler farmers for marketing.

All these employees live on the farm with their spouses and young children. The manager, who is Pule's relative, lives in the main farmhouse, while his own quarters, which consist of a much smaller house, are being built close by, on the eastern side of the main farmhouse. The crop foreman and the tractor driver, who are not related to their employer, live in two smaller two-roomed houses, about a hundred yards to the west of the main farmhouse. These houses are very close to one another, forming a workers' compound. Thus the expansion of living quarters under the local farmer in the post-settler era has retained the classical settler pattern where the living quarters of the farmer and the workers are separate.

During harvest times, occasional labourers are employed from the neighbouring villages.

The wages of Pule's employees on the cultivation side are high by the standards of individual farmers, settler or local, throughout the Tuli Block. The high wage levels on Pule's farm are attributable to his additional FAP grant which was specifically meant to cover wages. The crop foreman earns P350 per month, a wage level that is much higher than the P180 that Vorster, the largest and most successful of the resident settlers, pays his foreman. The tractor driver earns slightly less than the crop foreman but at P250 per month his salary is much higher than the P75 that he was earning for similar work on an Afrikaner-owned farm in the Transvaal, before he was recruited by Pule. The manager, typical of locals in the employment of their cousins, would not disclose his salary. But from appearances, he is also very well paid.

Despite all the evidence of strong financial backing, Pule projects an outlook of simplicity. Unlike the district elites he, along with other national elites, does not flaunt his wealth.

The focus now turns to the labour on Pule's farm. Kinship was a decisive factor in the hiring of the manager, Pule's cousin. Before recruiting him, Pule had tried to employ his own nuclear family members, but they objected, stating that he was trying to turn them into his slaves. They found it a tall order to be asked to take up employment in the individually owned property of someone with whom they shared the same genealogical position within their family. This point is developed in the analysis of kinship labour in locally-owned enterprises, in Chapter 5. The manager, who does not have secondary education, has no formal training in cattle ranching or crop production. The purpose of having such a manager, so closely identified with Pule and clearly dependent upon him, is to make Pule's presence felt, even in his absence. Everyone should be working according to Pule's wishes under the eyes of his stand-in. To facilitate his job as overall farm supervisor, the manager has been given a farm vehicle.

The discussion centres next on the two workers immediately below the manager. The crop foreman originally came from outside Botswana as an agricultural demonstrator in Botswana's Ministry of Agriculture. He was stationed in the communal areas adjacent to Pule's farm, and in due course got to know Pule. Having retired from service with the government, and awaiting a gratuity with which he intended to start an irrigation project on the banks of a river in the communal areas, Pule recruited him.

Although the crop foreman had wanted to be given charge of both livestock and crop production, and thus to be better paid, his job is limited to the production of crops: lucerne, maize and beans, on 12 ha. of land. The tractor driver has extensive experience in tractor ploughing, having worked for years in the Tuli Block and before then in the Transvaal from where he retired in the early 1980s to take up his present appointment on Pule's farm. He comes from a small settlement in the communal areas nearby.

When the dependent manager is around, the driver and the crop foreman appear jovial and cheerful. But when he is away, they raise many complaints, which relate to Pule's absenteeism. Their greatest complaint is that the delegation of authority to the manager by Pule, effectively hinders them doing their work in the way they have been taught during their training. The crop foreman wants to decide when and how to plant the first crop of beans, but that decision is made by Pule through his manager. The tractor driver insists on turning the soil before the rains, as he was taught by his previous white employers, but Pule does not allow him to do so. Pule agrees that it is useful but thinks it too expensive. These two workers also complain that Pule prefers to ask his untrained, and from their point of view, ignorant manager, for technical advice rather than consult them. As a result, the workers feel they are not working for their employer to the best of their ability.

The force of modern technology means that, unlike an ordinary arable field in the communal areas, under irrigation this farm produces two crops of maize and beans during the warm months of spring and autumn. The point is that here there are two cropping seasons in any year, whereas in the communal areas there is only one such season. In 1985, a total of 647 bags of maize were harvested. Lucerne is also grown under irrigation from the beginning of spring and harvested continuously until the following winter. Just like Charles the settler national elite who had a state contract to breed bulls on behalf of the government, Pule has a similar contract with the Ministry of Agriculture to grow special breeds of these crops on behalf of the state. His crops are bought by a government research station and not by the Agricultural Marketing Board which buys crops for the general public. But unlike the bull subsidy scheme which pays the producer what is considered a less than free market price, the agricultural research station pays its specialist crop producers special prices higher than the ruling prices at the Marketing Board.

In the rest of the country, there are other farmers who have similar contracts with the state, but in the Tuli Block, Pule has been, up to 1989, the only one. It is widely believed that this contract is the reason for his ever-increasing hectarage under irrigation. His future plans include the construction of a weir with the hired help of Verlem, Vorster's son, in order to increase the cultivation of beans, especially.

Pule's production of lucerne is not under the aegis of the research station but is a reflection of Pule's own initiative to reach out for profitable enterprises. Bales of lucerne, which must be a minimum of 250, are bought by the Botswana Livestock Development Corporation (BLDC) at P5 per bale. BLDC retails them to cattle producers for P2.50 per bale.

According to his own estimate, Pule had hoped that he would begin to break even in the 1986–7 agricultural season, making his first profit in the following year 1987–8. But a failure of rainfall in December 1986 resulted in very little water in the Limpopo river. Without irrigation, dry land farming on his thirty-acre cultivable land gave him a mere sixty bags of maize compared with the 650 bags of maize that he had harvested in January 1986. Pule's 1986–7 crop failure echoes the drought of the 1980s which has broken out in other parts of Africa (see Moris, 1987). It also illuminates the vulnerability of the newly settled local farmers, that is, the first generation farmers who have not yet developed a sophisticated infrastructure such as weirs, whereas the settlers have developed the necessary infrastructures and are thus better equipped to make the best use of even the lowest tide in the river, as Verlem's case, discussed under Vorster's profile, has indicated.

DIFFERENTIATION MECHANISMS BETWEEN NATIONAL AND DISTRICT ELITES

By and large, the differentiation mechanism between the district and the national elite is the privilege of office and the consequent access that such office holders have to restricted but crucial information. This privilege is the prerogative of national elites only. By law such information may not at certain times be made public, for instance during certain stages of policy formulation, those involved in the formulation of such policy are being able to take advantage of such knowledge before their competitors get to know about the policy. In fact, certain information that is crucial for the ranching business is kept from public knowledge until it appears in the form of a report at the end of the year. Such information includes changes in cattle prices, triggered by factors that are both internal and external to the BMC (Morrison, 1986: 36). It is those ranchers that are on the BMC Board of Directors who make the best use of such information, for example, by holding back cattle sales during the time in question.

Through an analysis of the Financial Assistance Policy, I show how the national elite exploit their privileged position for personal economic gain. The analysis of the Financial Assistance Policy is in effect an analysis of the operation of state bureaucracy. Unveiling the differentiation among national elites, it also shows they have both national and personal economic ambitions which are ingrained in the policies they formulate in their role as the national leadership. Such an approach which recognises the differentiation among national elites takes care of the criticism that the actor-oriented approach collapses individual interaction and intergroup interaction, eventually regarding the civil servant as the state (von Benda-Beckman et al., 1989: 217).

In a study of African capitalism, Kennedy asserts that office holders and politicians have sought private property and business interests through exploiting their privileged access to state resources, thereby creating what he calls parasitic capitalism (Kennedy, 1988: 67). A supportive statement from Long reports a similar situation in Latin America where dominant class interests, represented either directly or indirectly in state power were critical in determining the types of policies adopted by the state (Long, 1988: 112). The situation in Botswana seems to be in chorus with the foregoing, not only on the basis of the author's fieldwork among the entrepreneurs in eastern Botswana but also according to the observation of others. Writing about Botswana, Picard asserts that the primary beneficiaries of government policy in the areas of economic and rural development have been the organisational elites, bureaucratic, professional and political, who dominate the system (Picard, 1987: 264).

According to Ubels, the state initiates irrigation projects mainly for boosting export production, the production of food for national and regional markets, and for the stabilisation of rural areas (Ubels, 1989: 197). In Botswana, a stated additional goal is to reduce the country's reliance on food imports, especially cereals. In the process of formulating and implementing this policy, the national elite, the subject of this study, enhances his entrepreneurial role. It must be stressed, however, that neither the policy nor the manner in which it is implemented is in question here. The example merely serves to show how the system works to the advantage of those bureaucrats who formulate and implement the policy, and how the process puts their competitors, such as the district elite, not placed within the executive state machinery, at a disadvantage.

The Financial Assistance Policy is a creation of the post-colonial state meant to support individual and group projects which aim for the creation of industries and jobs. The industrialisation of arable agriculture is a main focus. Unlike the National Development Bank which, as a semi-autonomous public body, does not fall under any one government department, the Financial Assistance Policy is located within the Ministry of Finance and Development Planning. As such, it is administered by civil servants who work under the direct authority of the bureaucrats or the executive national elite. An executive national elite such as Pule has had two specific advantages: first he has been involved in the formulation of the Financial Assistance Policy and, second, he is currently involved in its implementation. His employment of a firm of accountants to support his application is an indication that he knows what it takes to produce the necessary information. Indeed the position he occupies within the state gives him the immense credibility which would probably be enough by itself to secure him the grant he needs. Nevertheless, to satisfy the requirements and therefore to safeguard the state, he produces an independently creditable report of the accountants.

Many others, including district elites, who protest at having been denied much smaller grants, perceive that the overwhelming reason for the granting of such a large sum of money to an executive national elite is the enormous power such an elite wields. Viewing the whole matter in perspective, it can be seen that district elites easily participate in the National Development Bank, an agency, but not so easily in the higher levels of the Financial Assistance Policy. In their quest for national resources they may beat many small farmers who fail to qualify for loans from the bank but they are not as well placed as the national executive elite to command sufficient power to have a share in the greater, more rewarding, but also more highly-placed, national funding packages.

Using only one example may distort the picture and it is important, therefore, to project the general picture by going beyond this one example. The utilisation of the Financial Assistance Policy at the high level may not be the preserve of the executive national elite as such. Although reliable statistical data is scant, it is common knowledge that like executive national elites, commercial national elites, mainly non-local, manage to participate at the highest level of the Financial Assistance Policy. In view of that, the general picture therefore is that with reference to local elites, this Policy is dominated by executive national elites but is not utilised exclusively by its members.

The fact that national elites in general can be used experimentally by the state to produce alternative crops and breeding stock on its behalf shows the greater privilege their positions can carry vis-à-vis the position of the members of the district elite. Table 4.1 below, which shows that the national elite has taken the larger share of the Financial Assistance Policy funds, substantiates the assertions made above with respect to the two kinds of elite as broad undifferentiated categories. Non elites are included in order to make a fuller comparison among all local farmers in the Tuli Block.

The table below shows that 50 per cent of national elites in the Tuli Block had small-scale Financial Assistance Policy grants. Only 27 per cent of district elites and 10 per cent of the non-elites had small-scale grants. It can be seen too that 30 per cent of national elites had medium-scale Financial Assistance Policy grants. No other category of Tuli Block farmers had medium-scale Financial Assistance Policy grants in 1989.

There are other categories of the national elite who, because they are not holding executive positions in the state, do not get as much from the Financial Assistance Policy as the executive national elite. That is because privileges of elites have both a specific as well as a general dimension, whether at the national or at the district level. The National Development Bank is an example of a general privilege of elites across different levels, while the Financial Assistance Policy at the level at which the executive national elite utilises it is an example of a specific privilege. The differentiation between the National Development Bank and the Financial Assistance Policy is in certain respects too general in that the real difference does not always match.

It must be stated that both financial institutions have various levels of participation, thereby enabling entrepreneurs of various standing to participate at different levels. Nevertheless, the analysis has demonstrated how the

TABLE 4.1: Distribution of Financial Assistance Policy grants by category and scale, 1989.

Category	Range					
	Small-scale P500–P25,000			Medium-scale P25,001–P100,000		
	A	B	C	A	B	C
National elite	5	10	50	3	10	30
District elite	4	15	27	0	15	0
Non-elite	1	10	10	0	10	0

A   Number of elites with FAP grants.
B   Total number of local elites in the Tuli Block.
C   A, as a percentage of B.

Source: Author's field data.

general and the specific dimensions of elite privilege also reflect the variation among elites in terms of the power they wield in the competition for national resources.

There is an important point that needs to be highlighted in the discussion of state supported entrepreneurial ventures. The point is that by supporting such ventures as the production of cereals, exotic cattle breeds, and the manufacture of malt, the state is actually promoting its own position in enterprise. The point has to be made that it is the state that compartmentalises specialisation in agricultural enterprise. Specialisation in the production of exotic breeds, a major emphasis in the production of certain crops, as well as emphasis in food manufacturing are all a response to state initiatives.

Although this is at the expense of some repetition, further analysis of certain issues that have already been raised is nevertheless crucial in order to create the context for illuminating more factors involved in differentiating among the local entrepreneurs in the Tuli Block. The analysis at this point is also in a position to shed light on the economic rationality behind certain actions of local entrepreneurs which are often misunderstood, such as the buying of expensive exotic bulls from South Africa by district elites, an action that has been reduced to status-seeking; or the apparent playing down of wealth by some national elites, which has been branded as hiding from public view the benefits of their office.

So far, I have illuminated the impact of the state in the mediation of local entrepreneurs through an analysis which has, among other things, also indicated the process through which the state is responsible for the differentiation among the elite. Also, as has been shown, that important though the state may be in the mediation of the local farmers, it may not be said to be altogether indispensable, since farmers are still able to run viable enterprises without its support. In fact, farmers who operate outside the framework of the state tend to evolve more viable enterprises than those who operate with its support. The enterprises of the latter usually collapse once state support fails.

PITSO – THE RESIDENT NON-ELITE LOCAL FARMER

Hitherto in this study, local farmers are part-time freehold farmers and also elites in their villages or places of full-time occupation. This is the case of a full-time local Tuli Block farmer who is also not an elite: a non-elite farmer, who, unlike those presented so far, is resident on his ranch, a full-time farmer. Pitso's case highlights the problem of an ordinary local farmer who expands into the Tuli Block with the aim of making his living from the farm. His farm is the main source of his livelihood, and not just one of his economic activities. He therefore realises that he has to make the full and best use of it, as it must provide him with his livelihood. This constrains him to live on his farm, in order that he should give it all the resources of his time and energy. Although his aim in buying the farm is to overcome his cattle straying which he has been experiencing at the cattlepost, his overall strategy of cattle production and perhaps also the small size of the farm, forces him to retain his cattlepost, where part of the herd has continuously to be kept.

In order to maximise the income from the farm, Pitso practises mixed farming, raising cattle and producing cereal crops. He also attempts, but without success, to produce vegetables for sale. His venture into horticulture is undermined by cheaper vegetables imported from South Africa. There is free trade between Botswana and South Africa because the two countries, along with Lesotho and Swaziland, belong to the same Customs Union. In other words, it is the policy of the state which defeats Pitso.

On a more general level, Pitso is faced with the problem of being a first generation farmer with a big farm mortgage to pay. The payment of the mortgage, his top priority, puts him under a tight financial squeeze, despite the fact that he is already undercapitalised. His financial squeeze is manifested partly in the structure of his herd which has no oxen (because they have had to be sold), and partly in his spartan way of life, which forces him to mediate in simplicity. Also, he is forced to run his small farm as a cattlepost, and makes no developments on the range or even repairs to the farm's perimeter fence and the house, which might be expected of a resident farmer such as himself.

Aged about sixty-five years, Pitso comes from a village fifty miles from his farm. He is married and has fifteen children. One of his grown up sons is a university graduate and is employed as an administration officer at the headquarters of the Ministry of Agriculture in the national capital. Unlike the rest of the local ranchers in this study, Pitso has never been to school, although he can read and write in the vernacular. He has never been in paid employment, apart from serving in World War II. His cattlepost, like that of Tau, is on the banks of the Shashi river, about twenty miles from his home village. A large portion of his herd is a dowry from his father-in-law.

In his own words, Pitso, who comes from a drought prone area, was attracted to the Tuli Block by the security of its perimeter fence and its assured water supply, following the drought of 1972–3. In the mid-1970s, he obtained a loan from the National Development Bank and bought his small farm of 500 hectares for P20,000. As soon as he had bought the farm, he settled on it, together with his wife and their dependent children. His main problem was to pay the mortgage. To raise money as quickly as possible he practised arable farming alongside cattle production. He produced cereals and vegetables. This was the most intensive strategy of expansion to be practised by a local farmer at the time. It is similar to that used by the early settlers, especially the Afrikaners. Vorster, a neighbour of Pitso's, who is generally critical of local farmers, especially Tau and Molema, commends

Pitso for his mixed farming strategy and believes that it will pull him through the drought of the 1980s and help him further towards economic expansion.

Cattle production remains Pitso's main farming activity, despite his mixed farming. Like most local farmers, he had no freehold ranching experience when he bought his farm. He gained the experience at a high cost. When he settled on the farm, he brought in all his cattle from the cattlepost. However, within a short time the farm was overgrazed. Next, Pitso withdrew half of the herd and transferred it back to his cattlepost, where it has been kept since. The structure of his herd which is kept on the farm, manifests the strain on his economy. The 120 head of cattle conspicuously lack oxen and old cows. Since 1985, his oxen and cows have been marketed at the rate of 10 per annum to pay the mortgage. On no other herd in the Tuli Block have I seen such a significant herd structure.

Run-down facilities lower the standard of farming on this farm. There are no paddocks since the fence poles are worn out. Cattle-drinking troughs are leaking, thereby wasting water and therefore engine oil as well. It can be said that, in common with his local neighbours, and perhaps for reasons which converge as much as they diverge, Pitso also practises limited animal husbandry. He de-ticks more irregularly than they and he keeps a limited stock of bovine medicines.

The drought of the 1980s has not been as disastrous for Pitso as it has been for his local neighbours. When it struck, at the end of 1979, he had a few head of cattle on the farm, having sold many of them since 1976 in order to pay the mortgage. Many of his cattle kept at the cattlepost died and he lost quite a few on the ranch. From 1981 to 1984, he could not sell because of the restrictions on cattle movement and the very poor conditions of the few that survived the drought. In 1981, when Pitso stopped the payment of his premiums of the mortgage, he had been left with only four years to complete the payment. But the drought set him back by another four years, leaving him with a total of eight years' balance to pay.

In 1985, following the moisture improvement in the northern Tuli Block, Pitso sold most of his fully grown cattle to the BMC, thus resuming the payment of the farm mortgage. He did not sell any cattle from his cattlepost. Rainfall had remained poor in the communal areas and there had not been enough grass at his cattlepost. He sold cattle once more at the beginning of 1986, once again from the herd on the farm.

Arable farming is the second most important economic activity on Pitso's farm. He cultivates mainly the cereals maize and sorghum, on four hectares. Alongside the cereals, he grows ancillary crops such as sweet reed, melons, beans, for sale as well as for home consumption. He has arable land in the communal areas, but since 1979 when the drought started, he has not planted anything on it. On his farm, he has been planting crops every year despite the drought. His problem, however, is that besides a tractor, he has no other farming implements.

Unlike Vorster the settler, Pitso, like Molema, uses traditional farming methods. Whereas Vorster uses the modern technique of row-planting when growing groundnuts, Pitso sows his cereals through the broad-casting method. He is quite aware that financial returns on groundnuts are much higher than they are on maize and sorghum but he lacks the advanced and expensive technology that is required to produce groundnuts on a large scale.

As a dryland farmer, Pitso cannot plant his crops in two seasons per calendar year as does Pule, an irrigator. Consequently, the cash returns per given unit of land are lower on his farm than they are on the farm of either the settler or the state elite. Notwithstanding that, the return on Pitso's farm is probably still above average on an equal area of cultivable land in the communal areas, given the high rate of crop failure in the communal areas during the drought. In 1985, Pitso marketed sixty bags of maize and forty bags of sorghum to a Botswana Agricultural Marketing Board depot in a nearby village, after putting aside enough food grain to last his large family until the following harvest season.

It is significant that even though Pitso's harvest was much smaller than that of the state elite who reaped over 600 bags of maize on 12 hectares, it was nevertheless much greater than that of the absentee 'village big man', Molema, who reaped only seven bags of corn on 2.5 hectares.

On Pitso's farm, as in the communal areas, most crops are consumed as soon as they ripen, well before the harvest. Such crops include maize, bean leaves, melons and sweet reed. After harvest, whatever remains of them is sold in an open market in the nearby town, some 30 miles away.

As soon as Pitso had settled on his farm, he grew vegetables such as cabbage and tomatoes under irrigation. He had intended to market them in a nearby town. And although he did not have much expertise in horticulture, he produced quite a good crop. However, in the town where he marketed them, the low prices of the vegetables imported from South Africa forced him out of business. He could not compete with South African vegetable imports because of the lower costs of mechanised large-scale production in that country. Faced with such a situation, Pitso discontinued horticulture.

The marketing of cattle and cereals presents a problem for Pitso who only has a one-ton pick-up van and a tractor but no trailer. The market for cereal crops is near his farm but the nearest market for other crops that he grows is thirty miles away. Lobatse, the home of the main Botswana Meat Commission abattoir, is 200 miles away. The distance from Pitso's farm to the nearest railway station is sixty miles. Trekking cattle for sixty miles, especially during a drought period, makes them lose condition.

In order to facilitate the marketing of his cattle and his crops, Pitso requested Financial Assistance Policy assistance to help him purchase a five-ton vehicle. Its price was P15,000 (£5,000). FAP turned down the request on the grounds that its assistance does not cover the purchase of vehicles for marketing livestock or ordinary crop produce. Pitso interprets this negative response as a reflection of his lower social status. He complains that the state gave Pule whatever he required, yet it cannot offer him a grant towards the purchase of an item that he desperately needs for his survival as a freehold farmer. He cannot see the difference between himself, a traditional farmer on commercial land and Pule, a commercial farmer on commercial land. His view is that since he is on commercial land, whatever economic activity he engages in is necessarily a commercial undertaking. Failure to make the distinction may be due to his limited education.

Labour use on Pitso's farm is unique; whereas virtually all other Tuli Block farmers use both family and hired labour, he uses family labour only. His two wives and his dependent children who live with him – these are his children who have not secured a place in secondary school – help him with all the farm work. As in the case of other Tuli Block farmers with grown-up working sons, those of Pitso's children who are now employed outside the farm, such as his graduate son, occasionally do errands for him. In particular, his graduate son, by virtue of his employment in the Ministry of Agriculture, may even help him with some valuable information which may boost the operations of the farm.

The use of only family labour on Pitso's farm is a reflection of both the small scale of production as well as the use of simple technology.

It can be seen, from the foregoing, that Pitso does not present any false image or flaunt his situation.

ELITES VIS-À-VIS NON-ELITES

It has been suggested that members of the district elite seem to play up their wealth, whereas members of the national elite tend to play down theirs. The comparison is further pursued by extending it to a local member of the non-elite. With neither the preoccupation to build up a reputation for himself, nor any intention to hide the benefits of a job, the non-elite has no reason to engage in what may be interpreted as the pretentious display characteristics of district elites. As such, he neither plays his wealth up nor does he play it down. Yet, his aims and actions remain complex. On certain occasions his actions resemble those of district elites, while on other occasions they resemble those of national elites. This seems to be inevitable since the action he follows occasionally brings together the opposite positions which are maintained by the two different levels of elite. In other words, the mediation of the non-elite occasionally brings together the different life-worlds of national and district elites.

To begin with the non-elite's priority of repaying the farm mortgage within the set time limit; this is not a priority of the district elite, of course, and indeed, the non-elite shares this priority with members of the national elite. Of course, given their privileged jobs, members of the national elite achieve their priority more easily than the non-elite. The fundamental difference, however, lies in the different reasons they have for the priority. If a non-elite failed to pay his mortgage, he would risk losing his income and the very source of his livelihood. Members of the district elite can afford to lose their farms because they are only part-time freehold farmers who have much of their assets and social credit outside the farms. A resident non-elite farmer has to make the payment of the mortgage a top priority because his expansion depends on his farm, and he has already invested in it.

To pursue this point, I consider the different cattle breeds found on the farms of the district elite on the one hand, and on the farm of the non-elite, on the other. While this issue is related to the importance of the farm in the entrepreneur's social life, it also goes beyond that and suggests a related consideration, the condition of the farm.

Consistent with their aim to improve their animal breeds and also perhaps to present themselves as the district nobility, district elites go to enormous expense buying exotic bulls from South Africa. The possibility of their aiming to raise their social image cannot be altogether ruled out. As Renfrew points out, actors manipulate material goods in order to gain prestige and higher status (Renfrew in Appadurai, 1986: 144). But, as was pointed out earlier, the reason for a particular display of lifestyle is to be found within the wider framework of the needs of the actor's mediation. National elites refrain from doing that. Although Botswana has strong trade links with South Africa, EC regulations forbid the sale of cattle originating from South Africa. This is because of the trade sanctions that some members of the Community currently maintain against that country. It is, therefore, government policy that all cattle bought from South Africa can be used only for breeding but not for resale. Since Botswana is keen to retain its place in the Community's beef market, this policy is closely implemented. In fact, a government minister, who is a national elite, was dismissed for contravening this policy. National elites are therefore reluctant to buy exotic breeds from South Africa, mainly perhaps because of avoiding allegations that can come from the public to which they market such animals in due course. This is yet another example showing that the failure of national elites to indulge in what is sometimes interpreted as prestige-seeking is precipitated by a desire to comply with bureaucratic norms and standards. Parson, who failed to appreciate the reason of the national elite for avoiding ostentatious mediation, termed their restrained conduct 'pretended simplicity' (Parson, 1979).

When a settler entrepreneur buys breeding animals from South Africa, he does it through his family firm in that country, so that he does not incur any expense through such action. The non-elite simply accepts that he has not the means to venture into the production of exotic breeds. Not only that, his overall perspective is different. Because his lifeworld spans the farm and the cattlepost, he is concerned to make sure that his herd must be composed of breeds which do well in both areas since he will occasionally need to move his cattle between both places. Knowing that exotic breeds do not always do well in the drought conditions of the eastern hardveld, he concentrates on the expansion of the indigeneous Tswana breed. Keeping only the Tswana breed is a common strategy among small-scale cattle producers in the communal areas. The Tswana breed is well known for its hardiness, an advantage in the dry conditions of eastern Botswana.

Nevertheless, prestige lies in the ownership and production of exotic breeds. The non-elite, by not attempting to produce exotic breeds, demonstrates his lack of interest, for the time being at least, in prestige-seeking. In his choice of a hardy and reliable breed, he is acting with an economic rationality that is like that of the executive national elite, and contrary to that of the local elite. From the point of view of villagers, the member of the non-elite has adopted the strategy of a small-scale rather than a large-scale cattle producer.

A related consideration for comparison is the condition of the farm, that is, its resources and management levels. The condition of the farm has, in the wider literature, become a virtual yardstick of the sophistication of the farmer (see reports on the Nojane farms in Botswana, and Overseas Development Institute publications on group ranches in Kenya, especially). If the condition of a farm were really a useful yardstick of sophistication, then virtually all local farmers would have to be labelled as unsophisticated, because their farms are in a run-down condition; the management levels are low because of the use of inexperienced herders who are transferred from the cattleposts. Under such circumstances, keeping an indigeneous herd, which is a strategy of the non-elite, is more in harmony with the farm condition, than is the breeding of exotic animals, a strategy of the district elites. Viewed in this light, the non-elite is therefore more rational than the district elite.

ABSENTEEISM VIS-À-VIS RESIDENCE

To turn to residence as against absenteeism the success of some national elites in repaying their farm mortgages depends upon their having a high and reliable off-farm income, secure against drought, and not just the privilege of position. It follows that while it is most advantageous for the non-elite to work and live on the farm, it is nevertheless also most advantageous, under the circumstances, for a highly-waged farmer to live away from the farm. Thus, the economic wisdom of living on or off the farm for locals depends on the farmer's portfolio of jobs, and particularly on the scale of off-farm income. In apparently different actions, which lead in opposite directions, farmers may act rationally, each according to the pattern of resources at his

TABLE 4.2: Comparison of crop produce between resident and absentee local farmers.*

| | Average number of bags of corn† produced per farmer | | | |
	1984–5	1985–6	1986–7	1987–8
Resident farmers	70	79	93	21
	(P1,260)	(P1,500)	(P1,860)	(P464)
Absentee farmers	0	0	7	36
			(P140)	(P756)

Notes:
* The national elite are excluded because one of them is a large-scale arable producer but an absentee farmer. The inclusion of his produce would unduly distort the difference between resident and absentee farmers in terms of crop produce.
† Corn includes maize, sorghum and beans. A bag is 70 kg of corn.
( ) Monetary value of corn.
Source: Author's field data.

disposal. Their diverse choices of options do not reflect a contradiction but, rather, a variation in strategies, occasioned by a variation in resources. Such variation in strategies leads to differences in agricultural systems. Eventually, the heterogeneity in agriculture becomes the systematic outcome of conscious and goal oriented strategies of the farmers.

To local farmers in general, Tuli Block farming is a secondary economic activity, and not the main one. Hence, they prefer to spend much of their time in the villages, at the capital or elsewhere, where they earn the greater part of their income, and where they are recognised as members of the elite. The same logic applies conversely to a farmer who is not of the elite, and there are quite a number of such farmers in the Tuli Block (see Table A.1b). Full-time residence on the farm and away from a home village is his preferred option, given his lack of alternative attractions and interests. In fact, he buys the farm in an attempt to make the economic breakthrough which he has failed to achieve on the open range. And just as members of the elite find they have to live in the places where they earn most of their livelihood, so does the non-elite find it necessary to live on the farm, which he perceives as his economic lifeblood.

An advantage of residence over absenteeism is that it can give the farmer an opportunity to diversify farm-based production.

Mixed farming can have the advantage of complementarity between crop production and cattle raising. In the case of the non-elite farmers resident on their farms, crop production significantly boosts their entire farming activity. They are able to earn money from it and also to provide their own food requirements. The difference is illustrated in Table 4.2.

Quite clearly, resident farmers make a significantly much higher income from arable production compared to their absentee colleagues. Such income is necessary to keep the farm going, in the absence of any other income apart from that from the cattlepost. Equally important, it is a tremendous saving of money for the farm to produce its own food requirements. Hence, it is not a waste or a sign of backwardness for the farm residents to consume part of the crop as it ripens, before the harvest. Indeed, self-sufficiency in food supply has been a fundamental principle of early freehold farming all over the world (see Bennett, 1979, for North America; Riviere, 1972, for North Brazil; Hodder-Williams, 1983, for Zimbabwe).

Residence and absenteeism bring about clearly different uses of labour. Absentee local farmers use extended family labour alongside hired labour. By contrast, the resident local farmer uses family labour exclusively. This point is emphasised below in the discussion of labour use among local entrepreneurs. There are two main considerations which the resident local farmer takes into account when selecting his option. The scale of farming, as well as the technology used, are important considerations in his use of inexperienced nuclear family labour. Given the small scale of traditional farming and the narrow range of diversification, his farm activities can be adequately done by his family labour. He therefore feels no need to hire extra labour. The second reason is his serious shortage of cash, which results from his lack of an off-farm income. Undercapitalised as he is, and desperately in need of money to do basic farm repairs, he could not afford to hire labour. Such action would jeopardise the fulfilment of his burning desire to pay the mortgage in time.

Using family labour, whatever the level of its skills, is another advantage that the non-elite farmer has over other local ranchers. It saves him money and gives him valuable capital needed for the day-to-day operation of the farm. Like his limited diversification, his use of family labour is another benefit of his resident status.

Residence has yet another advantage. It enables the farmer to ascertain personally that there is less wastage of resources. His own appearance of simplicity in dress and manner, and his unmistakable resourcefulness, together with the run-down condition of his farm, are all testimony to his fervent desire, his firm goal, to save as much as possible. He perceives that in his situation the expansion of his farm, in particular the payment of the mortgage, can be achieved more easily from within, i.e. through his residence on the farm. It is significant that the non-elite farmer is able to carry out his farming enterprise without any connection with the state except through the farm purchase loan obtained from the National Development Bank. This is an important point in that it shows that local enterprise is possible without assistance from the state and that entrepreneurs can still mediate without any links with the state.

5

CONCLUSION

This study has addressed the enterprise of ranching in eastern Botswana. In particular, the book has focused upon the socio-economic processes that are at work in ranching enterprises, shaping the actors into different kinds of entrepreneurs. In view of the lack of similar studies on ranching in Botswana, the concern first and foremost has been with providing an overall picture of ranching enterprises as they currently are in the Tuli Block. The aim has not been to make major policy recommendations about ranching. Nevertheless, a basis for certain policy recommendations has emerged in this study and these will be spelled out in this concluding chapter.

The argument about variation in ranch-based entrepreneurship has been built upon the detailed analysis of specific cases. It remains important to bring the underlying patterns into sharper focus, primarily with regard to plurality or specialisation of enterprise, social networks, and the interaction of the colonial and the post-colonial state.

Across the Tuli Block, the specific variation in ranches and ranch-linked enterprise is considerable. It might be thought that among settler ranchers the difference between Afrikaners and the English is the most salient. However, even among Afrikaner ranchers, there is as much variation as there is between them and the English. Nor is the situation any simpler among the local ranchers; there is considerable variation between the ranchers of the district and the national elite, as well as in relation to the ranch of the non-elite.

For purposes of exposition, the different aspects of the underlying patterns are presented in turn. It should be stressed, however, that these aspects, like the associated patterns as a whole, are inter-related.

To begin with the interaction between the colonial and the post-colonial state, that is the historical perspective. This dimension has re-affirmed that historical events across space are interrelated and it has been shown how settlement of the Tuli Block between the 1930s and the 1950s was linked to growing scarcity of agricultural land in neighbouring South Africa. Still within the historical perspective, it emerged that the opening of the Lobatse abattoir in 1956, an event that ended the prolific live cattle trade between Botswana, and, especially, South Africa, was a result of developments far away from Botswana. Britain, after running short of US dollars ceased importing beef from the United States, choosing instead to import it from its colonies which included Botswana. The result is that since 1956, the mediation of farmers has been largely determined by a policy that was formulated away from Africa.

The connection between the ranching enterprise and world events did not end with colonial rule. It has persisted into the post-colonial era. Since 1975, for instance, the ranching enterprise has been influenced by another major historical development, the creation of the EC which opened its beef market to Botswana at prices that have been deliberately made attractive. Botswana's ranching enterprise has benefited from the high beef prices paid by the EC market but at a high cost, even though it is necessary to accept that there is a positive aspect of the policy.

On another front, the transition to the post-colonial era has brought about the emergence of the modern elite at the expense of the traditional elite. That is because the political structures of the post-colonial era, democratic in nature, have shaken and challenged the traditional political structures and the traditional authority of the colonial period.

Next the focus is on the plurality and the specialisation of enterprise. It has emerged, throughout this work, that the viability of most Tuli Block farms depend, to some extent, on multiple entrepreneurship. Also, all the underlying patterns in this concluding chapter revolve around social networks. The ability of the entrepreneurs to take advantage of bordermanship, to enter into multiple enterprise, to derive benefits from the state and to get the best out of labour, have all hinged on the entrepreneurs' social networks. It has been possible for farmers without privileged office to obtain sensitive and valuable information through their social networks.

The importance of multiple enterprise in freehold farming was highlighted during the early years of freehold farming, and is well documented in the literature (see Osgood, 1929; Riviere, 1972, among others). It also features prominently in the archival material on early Tuli Block settler farming. Almost everywhere, including neighbouring South Africa (Grossman, 1988) and Zimbabwe (Mosley, 1983) the most successful farmers are those who have diversified their enterprises. In a country that is prone to drought such as Botswana, the need for diversification among farmers is even greater.

The family firms of settlers have pursued the alternative options of multiple enterprise and specialisation. It is the firm that pursues multiple enterprise that survives the drought, and even expands in the midst of drought, while the firm that chooses specialisation is liquidated during that same drought.

Multiple entrepreneurship of local farmers differs in form from that of the settlers. Among settlers, the farm is the hub of the multiple enterprise.

The farm is also the springboard for other economic activities, linked to the fact that most settlers live on their farms. On the other hand, local elites, who are absentee farmers, pursue village or urban economic activities which in most cases are not structurally connected with their farms, except in terms of resource distribution and re-allocation.

Another crucial underlying pattern in this study has been the notion of social networks. At a theoretical level, the notion of social network is closely related to that of lifeworld in the sense that both give an idea of the domain or broadness of the social space within which an entrepreneur mediates. Networks, as this study has clearly shown, are of different kinds. There are kinship networks, ethnic networks, and other kinds of connections which entrepreneurs forge such as with state officials or other entrepreneurs, patrons and clients. Entrepreneurs in this study have made use of various kinds of networks, sometimes simultaneously, to advance their enterprises. Those who have made use of the widest range of networks also seem to have been the most successful. More importantly, networks have enabled entrepreneurs to strategise viably outside the state domain.

Settlers with strong connections across the border have also relied on such connections for extension. Hence, a persistent theme in the success or failure of the Tuli Block entrepreneurs has been their ability to make full use of human resources within the wider society.

This study uncovers a major gap in the wider literature on social change, and not merely a gap in regional studies on southern Africa. Still at the beginning of our knowledge of certain transitional developments in entrepreneurship, such developments, about which far too little has been written, accompany the break-up of a settler monopoly, the formation of a new state, and the radical redirection of trade through change in the very nature of the international market. It might be thought that a further advance in explanation must depend upon having some general theory or grand framework, but, there is a prior need, one addressed by the author in much of this work – the description and analysis in some depth of specific types of entrepreneurial careers of family firms.

In the process of presenting and analysing the case material, a basis has emerged for some policy measures to be suggested for the attention of the Botswana establishment especially. They are presented below, not necessarily in the order in which they have appeared in the study.

The first policy measure relates to Botswana's decision to market its beef in the EC. There can be no doubt that this was a wise decision. Because the benefits for Botswana (for the farmers individually and the state) are enormous it is understandable that the EC insists on strict health measures as a condition for the entry of meat from Third World countries. Nevertheless, through cordon fences which hamper the much-required cattle movement across the country, the policy seems to defeat rather than facilitate ranching on the ground. No change to the policy is suggested here; rather, what is suggested strongly is a mechanism that will enable easy passage of livestock across the terrain while at the same time not compromising the high veterinary standards enforced by the fences. Such a mechanism might be effected through opening more points along the fences, even if this means more staff being recruited. The current effect of the policy, which leaves cattle frequently stranded behind fences and consequently overgrazing the range, should not be left unchecked.

The second policy measure concerns the possibility of restricting ranch owners to their ranches. For some time now, there has been a suggestion that people who own ranches should not be allowed to retain their rights to graze cattle in the communal areas. This study has shown that the implementation of such a suggestion would put ranch owners at a great disadvantage. Given the continuity between the ranch and the cattleposts, which is the situation among both settler and local ranchers, it would be virtually impossible to keep ranching as a viable enterprise. The evidence from this study, as seen in the cases of the Clark family firm and that of Tau, suggests that the difficulty of keeping the ranching enterprise viable would arise even in cases where ranchers tried to specialise in the production of exotic breeds.

Another relevant consideration, especially among the local ranchers, is that of the size of the farm. Most of them own very small ranches that could not sustain conventional ranching, under the present conditions of technology and management. Recurrent drought compounds and complicates the situation. Without access to the communal areas, which the ranchers use as something to fall back on, their ranching enterprises would never succeed. Also, it has been demonstrated that the local rancher is not concerned primarily with his ranch, but with his overall economic social being. The implication for that is that he has to integrate all his economic ventures, financially and geographically.

The third policy consideration is in the area of credit. In general, local farmers have purchased their ranches through loans obtained from the National Development Bank, a public credit institution. It is important that the state should assist locals to buy ranches and to improve animal husbandry as well as the quality of beef produced in Botswana, as is suggested in the next policy consideration below. Nevertheless, two points are worth noting in this regard: first, in Botswana, livestock production is already a subsidised economic undertaking. Second, the Tuli Block farms, like all freehold farms, are private property.

The study has pointed to the possibility of local farmers buying their farms for different reasons, not just for raising livestock. Also, it has been shown that, for various reasons, a prosperous farmer may give the impression that his ranching enterprise is making a financial loss. Molema's case has demonstrated that ranchers can siphon wealth from the ranch to the cattlepost.

This should not be taken to suggest that many local ranchers are dishonest. Yet, the constant movement of livestock by many local ranchers, in either direction between the farm and the cattlepost, does mean that Molema's case is representative of the average local rancher in the Tuli Block.

For that reason, public financial institutions such as the National Development Bank (NDB) need to exercise extreme care in their financial dealings with ranchers. Such institutions should know clearly, when granting a rancher a loan, whether they are financing livestock development in the Tuli Block or in the communal areas. Accordingly, the NDB has to apply a more rigorous screening procedure when it comes to granting loans for the purchase of these farms. Since it may be extremely difficult for the NDB to be sure of the real motive for a farmer buying a farm, it would appear that the best way to safeguard public funds is to ascertain that loans are repaid, irrespective of drought occurrence. Specifically, a loan used to purchase a freehold farm should not, under any circumstances, be written off as a bad debt.

The National Development Bank has recently shown a tendency to be strict with farmers who fail to pay up their loans in drought years. In 1992, the bank impounded agricultural equipment from farmers who had reneged on their debts in Barolong Farms, following a drought year. The same practice should apply to farmers who fail to repay their ranch purchase loans.

The fourth policy measure is in the area of setting up a minimum wage for agricultural workers hired by private individuals (and not by the state). In the late 1980s, Botswana decided to set a minimum wage for different jobs in the various sectors of the economy. In 1990–1 the government commissioned a study to establish whether or not there should be a minimum wage in the agricultural sector, for herders and arable workers employed by individual farmers either in communal or commercial areas (including freehold farms). Following the study, the government decided not to legislate a minimum wage in the agricultural sector. Meanwhile, this study has shown that, with the breaking up of the extended family, rights to what used to be family property, such as cattle, are being individualised. On the other hand, members of the extended family who now have individual rights to their cattle continue to use their relatives under norms which were in force before such family break-ups and the consequent individuation of property.

This means that within the setting of the extended family, the commoditisation of property (especially of cattle) has occurred at a faster rate than that of labour. In the process, people employed by their relations within the agricultural sector are not paid the corresponding market value of their labour; in spite of whatever payment in kind they receive, they end up being very much underpaid.

Social justice is a planning objective and guiding principle in the social development of Botswana. It is the responsibility of the government, therefore, to act in a manner that will remove the disadvantage suffered by people employed by their relations. In this respect, the legislation of a minimum wage for agricultural workers (relations and non-relations) on cattleposts, farms and arable lands is recommended.

The fifth recommendation addresses the production of exotic cattle breeds in the Tuli Block. It takes considerable resources to produce exotic breeds, as the case of the Clark family firm has exemplified. Yet there is a demand for such animals within the country, and it is also in the interests of Botswana that the demand can be supplied by local ranchers from within the country. For settlers during colonial times, ranching was a heavily protected and state-assisted economic venture. To that end, local ranchers who want to produce such breeds have to be supported by the state. The areas of support are in the marketing of breeds produced and in affording the ranchers credit facilities to start the process.

A recommendation that is related to the last is on the provision of extension services for local freehold farmers in general. The point has been made that ranching is not the main economic activity of local ranchers. It has been stressed too, that they do not seem keen to practice conventional ranching, partly because it would be expensive in comparison to raising cattle in the cattleposts. In spite of that position, it is necessary that the local ranchers, who are only first generation freehold ranch owners, be armed with thorough knowledge of conventional ranching, even if they do not appreciate it at this point in time. As the drought persists and as the national economic scene forces people's economic activities to be specialised, the knowledge of conventional ranching will become handy for local ranchers. Even at present, when they do not cherish or value such knowledge, it is more than likely that such ranchers could manage their cattle production better if they had it.

Provision of extension services to all ranchers in the freehold areas should be the responsibility of the state. The current position of the government is that since the colonial government gave more attention to freehold farms and comparatively less of it to the communal areas, the focus of public attention should now be on the communal areas, because, after all, it is in them that more livestock producers are to be found.

There is some merit in this argument. Nevertheless, the fact that commercial ranching requires great skill, especially for farmers not used to it, is something that the government's stand has not recognised. The fact that freehold areas have potential to improve quality beef production in Botswana, through producing exotic breeds, is another factor which the government does not seem to have taken cognizance of. In view of that, it is recommended that the state should support cattle production in the freehold areas through the provision of extension services.

Finally, there is the issue of lack of good road maintenance. Tuli Block farmers complain that the poorly maintained roads in their freehold area hamper their entrepreneurship. The complaint is genuine. However, it is difficult to justify the improvement of the roads in the Tuli Block with public funds while not simultaneously doing the same for roads at the cattleposts. But the Tuli Block also produces crops and manufactured food such as malt and this gives it a greater reason for its roads to be improved, in comparison with roads in the cattleposts.

As a way of supporting all forms of economic production in the Tuli Block, and in order to raise the potential of this place as an area of economic production, the post-colonial government should, as the colonial used to, provide a good maintenance service on all roads that serve it.

APPENDIX

METHODOLOGY

This study uses the actor-oriented approach with a strong interface element to investigate differential responses to changing social processes within the Tuli Block as a geographical locale, and between the Tuli Block and the wider society in Botswana. Using it, I describe the lifeworlds of the actors by establishing their different kinds of networks, based on kinship, trade, friendship and the actor's other associations with the society that he uses directly and indirectly to foster his enterprise. The interface dimension illuminates especially the way the actors struggle or negotiate with the intermediary structures of the state, namely its policy, the banks and extension services as agency, to modify the policies at the ground level in line with the development process as envisaged by the actors.

RESEARCH DESIGN

This study has treated the Tuli Block as one entity in which all farms were visited in order to establish the full variation among the farmers as reflected in the profiles. Altogether there were 183 farms of different sizes, owned by 19 farmers of English origin, 35 farmers of Afrikaner origin, 35 local farmers and 9 companies which could not be classified as Afrikaner, English or African (see Tables A.1a and A.1b). Of the 35 local farmers, 10 were classified as members of the national elite, i.e. they held senior public office in the national government, parastatal bodies or an elected position at the national level. Fifteen of the local farmers held relatively junior social positions at the district level as councillor, trader, public or company officer. The remaining 10 did not hold a high position and seemed to wield little influence in their society. As such, they constituted what I have termed the 'non elite farmers' in this study.

The different farmers were categorised by scale of cattle production, size of farm, level of elite status and type of entrepreneur. The level of status of an elite depended on whether one was a national or district elite. There exist variations within each of the three categories in Table A.1c above. This variation is discussed in the book. Most settlers are confined to their farms such that their lives do not penetrate the communal areas sufficiently to justify the application of the elite category to them. Nevertheless, their profiles cover the full range of variation within the above categorisation.

TABLE A.1a: Basic data on Tuli Block farmers.

	No. of farmers	No. of farms	Area (Ha.)	Av. area of land/farmer (Ha.)
Afrikaners	35	101	270,882	7,739
English	19	23	130,000	6,842
Locals	35	40	75,330	2,152
Companies	9	19	35,484	3,943
Total	98	183	511,696	20,676

Source: Compiled from various sources.

TABLE A.1b: Basic data on Tuli Block farmers (continued).

	Av. land/farmer (Ha.)	Av. no. of cattle per farmer	Hectares per animal
Afrikaners	7,739	1,019	8.0
English	6,842	1,384	5.0
Locals	2,152	(1,125)*	0.5
Companies	3,943	–	–
Tuli Block average	5,169	1,176	4.5

* Figure fluctuates between 750 and 1,500.
Source: Author's field data.

TABLE A.1c: Categorisation of local farmers by elite status.

National elite	Local elite	Non-elite	Total
10	15	10	35

Source: Author's field data.

BIBLIOGRAPHY

Allen, V. L., 1972. 'The meaning of working class in Africa', *Journal of Modern African Studies*, Vol. 10, pp. 169–89.

Almagor, U., 1982. 'Pastoral identity and the reluctance to change: the Mbanderu of Ngamiland', in R. P. Werbner (ed.), *Land Reform in the Making: tradition, public policy and ideology in Botswana*, Rex Collings, London.

Amin, S., 1972. 'Underdevelopment and dependence in black Africa – origins and contemporary forms', *Journal of Modern African Studies*, Vol. 10, No. 4.

Appadurai, A., 1986. 'Introduction: commodities and the politics of value', in A. Appadurai (ed.), *The Social Life of Things: commodities in cultural perspective*, Cambridge University Press, Cambridge.

Ayuko, L. J., 1981. *Organisation, Structures and Ranches in Kenya*, Overseas Development Institute, London.

Bailey, C. R., 1982. 'Cattle Husbandry in Botswana'. Unpublished Ph.D thesis, Cornell University, Ithaca.

Barnes, S. T., 1986. *Patrons and Power: creating a political community in metropolitan Lagos*, Manchester University Press, Manchester, for the International African Institute.

Barth, F. (ed.), 1963. *The Role of the Entrepreneur in Social Change in Northern Norway*, Norwegian Universities Press, Oslo and Bergen.

Barth, F. (ed.), 1967. 'Economic spheres in Darfur' in R. Firth, (ed.), *Themes in Economic Anthropology*, Tavistock, London.

Baxter, P. T. W., 1975. 'Some consequences of sedentarisation for social relationships', in T. Monod (ed.), *Pastoralism in Tropical Africa*, Oxford University Press, Oxford, for the International African Institute.

Baxter, P. T. W., 1985. 'From Telling People to Listening to Them: changes in approaches to the development and welfare of pastoral peoples'. Paper presented at the International Symposium on The African Horn, University of Cairo, January, 1985.

Baxter, P. T. W., 1987. 'The "New" East African Pastoralism'. (In press.) *Proceedings of a Symposium on the Exploitation of Domesticated Animals in Africa*, University of Aberdeen, April, 1987.

Behnke, R., 1983. 'Production rationales: the commercialisation of subsistence pastoralism', in P. Salzman (ed.), *Nomadic Peoples*, No. 14.

Bell, M., 1983. 'Inequality with growth in Botswana'. *Canadian Journal of African Studies*, Vol. 17.

Benda-Beckman, F. von, *et al.*, 1986. 'Interfaces and Janus-faces: a critical appraisal of the interface approach in development sociology from a socio-legal studies perspective', in N. E. Long *et al.* (eds), *The Commoditisation Debate: labour process, strategy and social network*. Papers of the Department of Sociology 17, Wageningen Agricultural University, Wageningen.

Benedict, B., 1968. 'Family firms and economic development', *South Western Journal of Anthropology*, Vol. 24, No. 1, Spring 1968.

Benedict, M. and Benedict, B., 1982. *Men, Women and Money in Seychelles*, University of California Press, Berkeley.

Bennett, J. W., 1979. *Northern Plainsmen, Adaptive Strategy and Agrarian Life*, Aldine Publishing Co., Illinois.

Benvenuti, B., 1975. 'General systems theory and entrepreneurial autonomy in farming', *Sociologica Ruralis*, 15 (1/2): 47–62.

Best, A., 1979. 'General trading in Botswana 1960–1978', *Economic Geography*, October 1979, pp. 598–612.

Beteille, S., 1974. *Studies in Agrarian Social Structure in India*, Oxford University Press, Oxford.

Bonacich, E., 1973. 'A theory of middlemen minorities', *American Sociological Review*, 38, pp. 583–94.

Botswana Government, 1942. *Botswana National Archives S.126 Council Minutes*, dd. 6.10.41, Mafeking.

Botswana Government, 1954. *Botswana National Archives S.103 Report of Legislative Council Minutes*, Mafeking.

Botswana Government, 1960. *Botswana National Archives S.126 Report of Legislative Council Minutes*, Mafeking.

Botswana Government, 1975. *The Tribal Grazing Land Policy*, White Paper No. 2 of 1975, Gaborone.

Botswana Government, 1977. *Rural Income Distribution Survey in Botswana 1974–5*, Gaborone.

Botswana Government, 1982a. 'Migration in Botswana: patterns, causes and consequences', *Final Report, National Migration Survey*, Gaborone.

Botswana Government, 1982b. *Presidential Commission on Economic Opportunities*, Ministry of Finance and Development Planning, Gaborone.

Botswana Government, 1985. *Animal Production Division*, Annual Report 1984/5, Ministry of Finance and Development Planning, Gaborone.

Botswana Government, 1990. *Household Income and Expenditure Survey*, Gaborone.

Box, L., 1986. 'Commoditisation and the social organisation of crop reproduction: conceptualisation and cases', in N. E. Long *et al.* (eds), *The Commoditisation Debate: labour process, strategy and social network*. Papers of the Department of Sociology 17, Wageningen Agricultural University, Wageningen.

Box, L., 1989. 'Knowledge, networks and cultivators: cassava in the Dominican Republic', in N. E. Long (ed.), *Encounters at the Interface: a perspective on social discontinuities in rural development*. Landbouwuniversiteit, Wageningen.

Chambers, R., 1983. *Rural Development: putting the last first*, Longman, London.

Cheater, A. P., 1983. 'Cattle and Class? Rights to grazing land, family organisation and class in Msengezi', *Africa*, 53 (4).

Cheater, A. P., 1984. *Idioms of Accumulation*, Mambo Press, Gweru.

Cliffe, L. and Moorson, R., 1979. 'Rural class formation and ecological collapse in Botswana', *Review of African Political Economy*, No. 15.

Colclough, C. and MacCarthy, S., 1980. *The Political Economy of Botswana*, Oxford University Press, Oxford.

Cohen, A. P., 1985. *The Symbolic Constitution of Community*, Ellis Horwood Ltd., Chichester, Sussex, England and Tavistock Publications Ltd, London.

Colson, E., 1968. *Planned Change: the creation of a new community*, University of California, Berkeley.

Comaroff, J. L., 1982. 'Class and culture in a peasant economy: the transformation of land tenure in Barolong', in R. P. Werbner (ed.), *Land Reform in the Making*, Rex Collings, London.

Croston, J., 1989. 'The Socio-economic History of Freehold Farms in Bechuanaland Protectorate 1903–1966'. Unpublished Ph.D research proposal.

Curtain, C., 1986. 'The peasant family farm and commoditisation in the West of Ireland', in N. E. Long *et al.* (eds), *The Commoditisation Debate: labour process, strategy and social network*. Papers of the Department of Sociology 17, Wageningen Agricultural University, Wageningen.

Douglas, S. P. S. and Craig, C. S., 1983. *International Marketing Research*, Prentice-Hall, Englewood Cliffs.

Duggan, W. R., 1983. 'Botswana's rural economy', in M. A. Ooman (ed.), *Botswana's Economy Since Independence*, Tataw-McGraw-Hill Publishing Co. Ltd, New Delhi.

Eakes, M. D., 1978. *Crop Pricing and Protection in Botswana*, Ministry of Agriculture, Gaborone.

Eakholm, E. and Brown, L. R., 1977. *Spreading Deserts: the hand of man*, United Nations Environmental Project Paper No. 13, Washington, DC.

Ettinger, S., 1972. *South Africa's Weight Restrictions on Cattle Exports from Bechuanaland 1924–1941*, Botswana Notes and Records, No. 4, Gaborone.

Firth, R. (ed.), 1967. *Themes in Economic Anthropology*, Tavistock, London.

Frank, A. G., 1967. *Capitalism and Underdevelopment in Latin America*, Monthly Press Review.

Frankenberg, R., 1967. 'Economic anthropology', in R. Firth (ed.), *Themes in Economic Anthropology*, Tavistock, London.

Freehold, D. M., 1977. 'The post-colonial state and its Tanzanian version', *Review of African Political Economy*, No. 8, April.

Gabatshwane, S. M., 1961. *Tshekedi Khama of Bechuanaland*, Oxford University Press, Oxford.

Galaty, J. G., Aronson, D. and Salzman, P. C. (eds), 1981. *The Future of Pastoral Peoples*, Institute of Development Studies, Nairobi, and Commission on Nomadic Peoples, Ottawa.

Giddens, A., 1984. *The Constitution of Society*, Basil Blackwell, Oxford.

Giddens, A., 1987. *Social Theory and Modern Sociology*, Basil Blackwell, Oxford.

Gilbert, S., 1973. 'The survival of chieftaincy in Botswana', *African Affairs*, Vol. 72, No. 287, April.

Goach, T., 1979. *An Experiment with Group Ranches in Upper Volta*, Overseas Development Institute, London.

Goldschmidt, W., 1980. 'An Anthropological Approach to Economic Development', in J. G. Galaty *et al.* (ed.), *The Future of Pastoral Peoples*, Institute of Development Studies, Nairobi, and Commission on Nomadic Peoples, Ottawa.

Grossman, D., 1988. 'Relations between Ecological, Sociological and Economic Factors affecting Ranching in the North-western Transvaal', unpublished Ph.D thesis, University of the Witwatersrand, Johannesburg.

Gulbrandsen, O., 1984. *When Land Becomes Scarce: access to agricultural land and communal land management in eastern Botswana*, University of Bergen, Bergen.

Gulbrandsen, O., 1987. *Privilege and Responsibility: on transformations of hierarchical relations in a Tswana society*, University of Bergen, Bergen.

Gulbrandsen, O., 1989. *Spatial Organisation and Hierarchy in a Tswana Society*, University of Bergen, Bergen.

Harvey, C., (ed.), 1981. *Papers on the Economy of Botswana*, Heinemann, London.

Heijdra, H., 1989. 'Social encounters and interfaces between farmers and intervening actors: the emergence of local organisation in western Mexico', in N. E. Long (ed.), *Encounters at the Interface: a perspective on social discontinuities in rural development.* Landbouwuniversiteit, Wageningen.

Helland, J., 1978. *An Anthropologist's View of Group Ranch Development*, International Livestock Centre for Africa, Nairobi.

Helland, J., 1980. 'Pastoralists and the Development of Pastoralism', Occasional Paper No. 20, African Savannah Studies, University of Bergen, Bergen.

Her Majesty's Stationery Office, 1960. *Report of an Economic Survey Mission, Basutoland, Bechuanaland Protectorate, Swaziland*, London.

Hitchcock, R., 1978. *Kalahari Cattleposts: a regional study of hunter-gatherers, pastoralists and agriculturalists in the Western Sandveld region, Central District, Botswana*, Ministry of Local Government and Lands, Gaborone.

Hitchcock, R., 1982. *Botswana's First Livestock Development Project and its Future Implications*, National Institute for Research, Gaborone.

Hodder-Williams, R., 1983. *White Farmers in Rhodesia 1965–1980*, Macmillan, London.

Hubbard, M. E. V., 1983. 'Botswana and the International Beef Trade: 1900 to 1981', unpublished Ph.D thesis, University of Sussex, Brighton.

Hunt, D., 1983. 'Chayanov's model of peasant household resource allocation', *Journal of Peasant Studies*, Vol. 10, No.2.

Ingold, T., 1980. *Hunters, Pastoralists and Ranchers: reindeer economies and their transformations*, Cambridge University Press, Cambridge.

Institute for Development Anthropology, 1980. *The Workshop on Pastoralism and African Livestock Development*, New York.

Janvry, A. de, 1981. *The Agrarian Question and Reformism in Latin America*. John Hopkins University Press, Baltimore and London.

Jarman, I. and Kutler, K. E., 1971. *Livestock Management and Production in the Kalahari*, Botswana Notes and Records, No. 4, Vol. 4, Gaborone.

Kabagambe, J. C., 1985. *Labour Utilisation in the Swazi Homestead*, Department of Sociology, University of Swaziland, Mbabane.

Kennedy, P., 1988. *African Capitalism: the struggle for ascendancy*, Cambridge University Press, Cambridge.

Kerven, C., 1977. 'Underdevelopment, Migration and Class Formation in the North East District of Botswana', unpublished Ph.D thesis, University of Toronto, Toronto.

Khama, S. T., 1971. *Traditional Attitudes to Land and Management of Property with Special Reference to Cattle*, Botswana Notes and Records, No. 4, Vol. 4, Gaborone.

Kitching, G. N., 1972. 'The concept of class in the study of Africa', *African Review*, No. 2, pp. 327–50.

Kostas, Y., 1977. 'Capitalism and peasant production', *Journal of Peasant Studies*, Vol. 5, 1977–8, pp. 448–57.

Kuper, A., 1975. 'The social structure of the Sotho-speaking peoples of Southern Africa', *Africa*, Vol. 1, No. 45.

La Clau, E., 1971. 'Feudalism and capitalism in Latin America', *New Left Review*, 74.

Landell-Mills, P. M., 1971. 'The 1969 Southern Africa Customs Agreement', *Journal of Modern African Studies*, Vol. 9, No. 2, pp. 263–82.

Lethola, L. L., Buck, N. G. and Light, D. E., 1983. *Beef Cattle Breeding in Botwana*, Botswana Notes and Records, Vol. 15, Gaborone.

Lévi-Strauss, C., 1963. *Structural Anthropology*, Basic Books, New York.

Leys, C., 1975. *Underdevelopment in Kenya*, University of California Press, Berkeley.

Litshauer, J. and Kelly, W. F., 1979. *The Structure of Traditional Agriculture in Botswana*, Ministry of Agriculture, Gaborone.

Little, P. D. 1984. 'Critical socio-economic variables in African pastoral livestock development', in J. Simpson (ed.), *Livestock Development in Sub-Saharan Africa*, Westview, Boulder, Colo.

Livingstone, I., 1971. *Economic Rationality among Pastoral Peoples: myth or reality?*, University of London Press, London.

Long, N. E., 1968. *Social Change and the Individual: a study of the social and the religious responses to innovation in a Zambian rural community*, Manchester University Press, Manchester, Manchester.

Long, N. E., 1972. *Kinship and Associated Networks among Transporters in Rural Peru: the problem of the local and the cosmopolitan entrepreneur*, University of Durham, Durham.

Long, N. E., 1979. 'Multiple enterprise in the central highlands of Peru', in S. M. Greenfield, A. Stricken and R. T. Aubey (eds), *Entrepreneurs in Cultural Context*, University of New Mexico Press, Albuquerque, New Mexico.

Long, N. E., 1984. 'Creating Space for Change: a perspective on the sociology of development'. Inaugural lecture for professorship of empirical sociology of non-western countries, 15 November, Wageningen Agricultural University, Wageningen.

Long, N. E., 1986. 'Commoditisation: thesis and antithesis', in N. E. Long *et al.* (eds), *The Commoditisation Debate: labour process, strategy and social network*. Papers of the Department of Sociology 17, Wageningen Agricultural University, Wageningen.

Long, N. E., 1988. 'Sociological Perspectives on Agrarian Development and State Intervention', in A. Hall and J. Midgley (eds), *Development Policies: sociological perspectives*, Manchester University Press, Manchester.

Long, N. E. (ed.), 1989. *Encounters at the Interface: a perspective on social discontinuities in rural development*. Landbouwuniversiteit, Wageningen.

Long, N. E. and Arce, A., 1987. 'The dynamics of knowledge. Interfaces between Mexican agricultural bureaucrats and peasants: a case study from Jalisco', *Boletin de Estudios Latino americanos I del Caribe* 43, diciembre.

Long, N. E. and van der Ploeg, J. D., 1988. 'New challenges in the sociology of rural development: a rejoinder to P. Vandergeest', *Sociologia Ruralis*, 1988, Vol. XXVII-1.

Long, N. E., van der Ploeg, J., Curtin, C. and Box, L. (eds), 1986. *The Commoditisation Debate: labour process, strategy and social network*, Papers of the Department of Sociology, 17, Wageningen Agricultural University, Wageningen.

Long, N. E. and Richardson, P., 1978. 'Informal sector, petty commodity production and the social relations of small scale enterprise', in U. J. Clammor, *The New Economic Anthropologist*, Macmillan, London.

Long, N. E. and Roberts, B. R. (eds), 1978.*Peasant Cooperation and Capital Expansion in Central Peru*, Institute of Latin American Studies, University of Texas, Austin.

Long, N. E. and Villareal, M., 1989. 'The changing lifeworlds of women in a Mexican ejido: the case of beekeepers of Ayuquila and the issue of intervention', in N. E. Long (ed.), *Encounters at the Interface: a perspective on social discontinuities in rural development*, Landbouwuniversiteit, Wageningen.

Mahoney, N. J., 1977. 'Birwa Traders and Neighbours', unpublished Ph.D thesis, University of Manchester, Manchester.

Manungo, K. D., 1977. 'The Role Of The Native Council In The Colonial Administration of Bechuanaland', B.A. dissertation, University of Botswana, Gaborone.

Massey, D., 1980. 'The changing political economy of migrant labour in Botswana', *South African Labour Bulletin*, Vol. 5, No. 5.

Mazonde, I. N., 1987. 'The Development of Ranching and Economic Enterprise in Eastern Botswana', unpublished Ph.D thesis, University of Manchester, Manchester.

McCartney, W. J. A., 1978. 'Local Government and the Politics of Development in Botswana', unpublished Ph.D thesis, University of Edinburgh, Edinburgh.

Meillassoux, C., 1978. 'The social organisation of the peasantry', *Journal of Peasant Studies*, Vol. 1, pp. 81–90.

Millar, J. R., 1970. 'A reformulation of A. V. Chayanov's Theory of the Peasant Economy', *Economic Development and Cultural Change*, 18, pp. 219–29.

Molutsi, P., 1986. 'Social Stratification and Inequality in Botswana: issues in development 1950–1985', unpublished Ph.D thesis, University of Oxford, Oxford.

Morapedi, N. T. (ed.), 1985. *Food Comes First: seminar proceedings on livestock production, marketing, training and development*, National Institute for Research, Gaborone.

Moris, J., 1987. *Coping with African Drought*, Overseas Development Institute, London.

Morrison, S., 1986. *Dilemmas of Sustaining Parastatal Success: the Botswana Meat Commission*, Institute of Development Studies Bulletin, 17, University of Sussex, Brighton.

Mosley, P., 1983. *The Settler Economies: studies in the economic history of Kenya and Southern Rhodesia, 1900–1963*, Cambridge University Press, Cambridge.

O'Connor, J., 1975. *The Fiscal Crisis of the State*, Macmillan, London.

Odell, M., 1980. *Planning for Agriculture in Botswana: a report on the arable lands survey*, Institute of Development Management, Research Paper No. 7, Gaborone.

Ooman, M. A. (ed.), 1983. *Botswana's Economy Since Independence*, Tata-McGraw-Hill Publishing Co. Ltd, New Delhi.

Osgood, E. S., 1929. *The Day of the Cattleman*, University of Chicago Press, Chicago.

Paine, R., 1971. 'A theory of patronage', in R. Paine (ed.), *Patrons and Brokers in the East Arctic*, Institute for Economic and Social Research, Memorial University of Newfoundland.

Parson, J., 1977. 'Cattle, class and the state in rural Botswana', *Journal of Southern African Studies*, vol. 7, No. 2, April.

Parson, J., 1979. 'The Political Economy of Botswana: a case in the study of politics and social change in post-colonial societies', unpublished Ph.D thesis, University of Sussex, Brighton.

Peters, P., 1983. 'Cattlemen, Boreholes, Syndicates and Privatisation in Kgatleng District of Botswana: an anthropological history of the transformation of the commons', unpublished Ph.D thesis, Boston University, Boston.

Peters, P., 1985. 'Transformations and Struggles in the Grazing Lands of Botswana'. Draft paper presented at a workshop on 'Anthropology and History in Modern Africa', Harvard University, June 2–3.

Phimister, I. R., 1978. 'Meat and monopolies: beef cattle in Southern Rhodesia 1890–1938', *Journal of African History*, XIX, 3, pp.391–414.

Picard, L. A., 1980. *Bureaucrats, Cattle and Public Policy: land tenure changes in Botswana*, University of Nebraska Press, Nebraska.

Picard, L. A., 1987. *The Politics of Development in Botswana: a model for success?*, Lynne Rienner Publishers, Boulder and London.

Ploeg, J. D. van der, 1986. 'The agricultural labour process and commoditisation', in N. E. Long *et al.*, *The Commoditisation Debate: labour process, strategy and social network*. Papers of the Department of Sociology 17, Wageningen Agricultural University, Wageningen.

Ploeg, J. D. van der, 1989. 'Knowledge systems, metaphor and interface: the case of potatoes in Peruvian highlands', in N.E. Long (ed.), *Encounters at the Interface: a perspective on social discontinuities in rural development*, Landbouwuniversiteit, Wageningen.

Ploeg, J. D. van der, 1990. *Labour, Markets and Agricultural Production*, Westview, Boulder, Colo.

Rampa, J., 1978. 'The Attempted Incorporation of Bechuanaland into South Africa', B.A. dissertation, University of Botswana, Gaborone.

Renfrew, C., 1986. 'Varna and the emergence of wealth in pre-historic Europe', in A. Appadurai, (ed.), *The Social Life of Things: commodities in cultural perspective*, Cambridge University Press, Cambridge.

Reyna, S. P., 1983. 'Dual class formation and agrarian underdevelopment: an analysis of the articulation of production relations in Upper Volta', *Canadian Journal of Agricultural Studies*, Vol. 17. No. 1.

Riviere, P., 1972. *The Forgotten Frontier: ranchers of northern Brazil*, Rinehart and Winston Inc., New York.

Roe, E., 1980. 'Development of Livestock, Agriculture and Water Supplies in Botswana before Independence: a short history and policy analysis', Cornell University, Paper No. 10, Ithaca.

Russell, M. and Russell, M., 1979. *Afrikaners of the Kalahari: a white minority in a black state*, Cambridge University Press, Cambridge.

Salzmann, P.C. (ed.), 1980. *When Nomads Settle: processes of sedentarisation as adaptation and response*, Praegor Publishers, New York.

Samboma, L., 1982. *A Survey of the Tuli Block Farms*, Ministry of Agriculture, Gaborone.

Samoff, J., 1979. *The Bureaucracy and the Bourgeoisie: decentralisation and class structure in Tanzania. Comparative studies in society and history*, papers of the University of Dar es Salaam No. 21, Dar es Salaam.

Sanford, S., 1980. *Keeping an Eye on the TGLP*, National Institute for Research, Gaborone.

Sanford, S., 1982. *Livestock in the Communal Areas of Zimbabwe: a report prepared for the Ministry of Lands: resettlement and rural development*, Overseas Development Institute, London.

Sanford, S., 1983. *The Design and Management of Pastoral Development*, Overseas Development Institute, London.

Serema, L., 1985. 'The foreign marketing structure of the Botswana Meat Commission', in N. T. Morapedi (ed.), *Food Comes First: seminar proceedings on livestock production, marketing, training and development*, National Institute for Research, Gaborone.

Shaine, D. R., 1986. *Hoofprints on the Forest: cattle ranching and the destruction of Latin America's tropical forests*, Institute of the ISHI, Philadelphia.

Sillery, A., 1952. *A Short History of Bechuanaland Protectorate*, Oxford University Press, Oxford.

Simpkins, C., 1975. 'Labour in Botswana', *South African Labour Bulletin*, 2 (5), pp. 28–35.

Stevens, M., 1969. 'Botswana's Geographical and Economic Position in a Politically Divided Southern Africa', paper presented at a conference on 'Economic Aid to Independent Southern African States' held 15–25 September in London.

Thothe, B. K., 1985. 'National Development Banks' credit assistance to livestock farming', in N. T. Morapedi (ed.), *Food Comes First: seminar proceedings on livestock production, marketing, training and development*, National Institute for Research, Gaborone.

Tlou, T., 1974. *The Nature of Botswana States: towards a theory of traditional government*, Botswana Notes and Records, Vol. 6, Gaborone.

Tyson, M., 1978. *The Rainfall Distribution in Botswana and Southern Africa*, Botswana Notes and Records, Special Edition, 1978, Gaborone.

Ubels, J., 1989. 'Irrigation systems as social interfaces: towards an understanding of irrigation development as an interactional process', in N. E. Long (ed.), *Encounters at the Interface: a perspective on social discontinuities in rural development*, Landbouwuniversiteit, Wageningen.

Vandergeest, P., 1988. 'Commercialisation and commoditisation: a dialogue between perspectives', *Sociologia Ruralis*, 1988, Vol. XXVIII-1.

Veenendaal, E. M. and Opschoor, J. B., 1986. *Botswana's Beef Exports to the EC*, Institute of Environmental Studies, Free University of Amsterdam, Amsterdam.

Vincent, V. and Thomas, R. G., 1960. *Agro-ecological Survey of Southern Rhodesia*, Government Printer, Harare.

Vries, P. de, 1990. 'Continuous Initiators: community and bureaucracy in the social construction of development in the frontier', paper written for the advanced research seminar, Wageningen Agricultural University, Wageningen.

Weber, M., 1964. *The Theory of Social and Economic Organisation*, Free Press, New York.

Weimer, B., 1984. 'Rich Farmers – Poor Environment: the economy and ecology of beef production in Botswana and West Germany', *Afrika Spectrum*, No. 3, pp. 253–67, Hamburg.

Wellington, J., 1932. 'Pioneer settlement', *American Geographical Society*, Special Publication, No. 14, 1932.

Werbner, P., 1987. 'Pakistani traders in a British city', in J. S. Eades (ed.), *Migration, Workers and the Social Order*, Tavistock Publications, London.

Werbner, R. P., 1988. 'From Heartland to Hinterland: elites and the geo-politics of land in Botswana', paper presented at the 15th annual symposium on Land in African Agrarian Systems, Center for African Studies, University of Illinois, Urbana-Champaign.

Werbner, R. P. (ed.), 1982. *Land Reform in the Making: tradition, public policy and ideology in Botswana*, Rex Collings, London.

Wylie, L., 1982. *Migrants to Freehold Farms in Botswana*, Government Printer, Gaborone.

Young, M., 1979. 'Influencing land use in pastoral Australia', *Journal of Arid Environment*, Vol. 2, pp. 279–88.

Zimbabwe Government, 1972. *Agro-economic Survey of South Western Matebeleland*, a report by the Agricultural Development Authority, Harare.

Zimbabwe Government, 1985. *Commercial Agriculture in Zimbabwe*, Annual Report, Ministry of Agriculture, Harare.

INDEX

EU Authorised Representative: Easy Access System Europe Mustamäe tee 5

0, 10621 Tallinn, Estonia gpsr.requests@easproject.com

Printed and bound by CPI Group (UK) Ltd, Croydon, CR0 4YY

16/04/2025

01846986-0002